SOFTBALL HITTING
FAST AND SLOW PITCH

BY
TOM PETROFF

With
Jack Clary

The Athletic Institute
North Palm Beach, FL 33480

Library of Congress Catalog Card Number 89-82615
ISBN 0-87670-120-9

A Word from the Publisher

This Sports Publication is but one item in a comprehensive list of sports instructional aids, such as video cassettes and 16 mm films, which are made available by The Athletic Institute. This book is part of a master plan which seeks to make the benefits of athletics, physical educational and recreation available to everyone. To obtain a free catalog, please write to the Athletic Institute at the address listed on the copyright page.

The Athletic Institute is a not-for-profit organization devoted to the advancement of athletics, physical education and recreation. The Institute believes that participation in athletics and recreation has benefits of inestimable value to the individual and to the community.

The nature and scope of the many Institute programs are determined by a Professional Advisory Committee, whose members are noted for their outstanding knowledge, experience and ability in the fields of athletics, physical education and recreation.

The Institute believes that through this book the reader will become a better performer, skilled in the fundamentals of this fine event. Knowledge and the practice necessary to mold knowledge into playing ability are the keys to real enjoyment in playing any game or sport.

John D. Riddle
President and Chief Executive Officer
The Athletic Institute

James Hotchkiss
Executive Director
The Athletic Institute

Acknowledgments

I'd like to thank the many persons who helped make this book possible: For their capable work as demonstrators, Lisa Gilbey of Mercer County Community College and Alex Usarzewicz of Rider College; for helping to select the demonstrators and providing the facilities for our photography sessions, coaches Bill Drake and Sonny Pittaro; for his work as my collaborator, Jack Clary; and for their shepherding the project from concept to finished books, the folks at Mountain Lion, Inc., especially John Monteleone, Martha Wickenden, and Joan Mohan.

Tom Petroff

Table of Contents

Foreword

Softball is a sport for the masses.

It knows no gender because softball has become the women's counterpart for baseball. Yet millions of men are part of recreational slow-pitch or fast-pitch teams. There are thousands of men's and women's leagues around the nation.

It knows no age because little children begin playing in PeeWee Leagues, and adults stay with it into old age.

It also knows no national boundaries because nations around the world have begun to adopt it as one form of the American baseball game in which everyone can participate. Look for it as part of the gold medal women's competition in the Olympic Games.

Softball is found everywhere. During Jimmy Carter's presidency, the softball games between his executive staff and the media who covered the White House were famous, not only because the President himself was a participant, but because the games were hard-fought, give-no-quarter affairs where two proud adversaries in the nation's business were not about to concede anything on the playing field, either.

America's youth have grown up knowing that "playing ball" is as much a part of their culture as television, radio, summer vacations, picnics and Santa Claus. Many will begin with slow-pitch softball, and then when old enough, graduate to baseball (hardball) or fast-pitch softball and stay with that for as long as their talent and physical abilities enable them to compete. Eventually, they will, if the love of the game burns as brightly, return to slow-pitch softball, where they can derive enjoyment for the rest of their lives.

There is nothing wrong with playing the game just to have fun, but the better your skills are, the more fun you'll probably have. This book is going to show you how to be a top-notch hitter, and isn't hitting really the reason why everyone plays the sport? While you're out in the field, aren't you waiting impatiently to get back and have the opportunity to hit?

Hitting a softball is not as easy as it may look—especially not in a fast-pitch game where the ball travels just about as fast as in baseball, but over a lesser distance. It requires a definitive grounding in solid hitting principles, because, believe me, if you ever have watched the fast-pitch game at its highest level, hitting a ball—even a large softball—is no easy task.

Part of any sport is disciplining oneself to learn the particular techniques. Then they must be practiced diligently so that the skill

levels are increased to their utmost. Softball—even slow-pitch softball—is no different.

This book will attempt to make that process easier by introducing
new techniques that will make you aware of proper (and improper)
body positions without having to be told. This can eliminate much of
the verbalization that goes into teaching, thereby getting rid of the
problems that arise when players interpret the wrong connotations of
words.

Proper techniques can be achieved by relying on one's senses—
seeing, touching, and feeling from within—through a series of "feel
points" found in the joints and muscles used in the hitting motion.

The feel points serve as a guide for correct practice because they
provide feedback from the body itself. After you learn them, no coach
need be present. Your biggest aids will be your body and perhaps a
mirror in which you can see what the proper form should be and then
recheck later to see if it is being carried through. The result can be a
process of sensory and visual recall instead of one based on words,
and this retention pocess will refine and reinforce good hitting habits.

While we talk principally about techniques in this book, let me
underscore the necessity to approach any team sport with the idea
that the "team" is Number One. Skills should be refined and polished
to help the team, and all attention should be paid to doing what is
necessary during a game to help the team be successful. With team
success will come individual success; sole concern over individual
success takes fun from the game and robs the participant of a real
purpose for playing.

In the same vein, the word "hustle" must be a part of your
program. Physically, it means giving your best effort; mentally, it
means being completely engrossed while on the field and knowing
precisely what you will do on each play. Hustle often comes with the
individual player, but it is developed in practice and utilized during a
game. It requires physical momentum such as sprinting onto the field
when your team's at bats are over and sprinting off the field when it is
time to resume them. It means every player, whether in the dugout or
on the field, knowing exactly what should be happening on every
play; being prepared for a role after each hit or out; and being willing
to do anything possible for the betterment of the team.

When you look at all of that, it really is a mind-set that will help you
take the principles of hitting from this book and apply them to
improving your own game. This mind-set will help you to stay in the
spirit of the game and your team...and enjoy for all time a sport that
is an absolute joy to play.

Tom Petroff
Iowa City, Iowa

I. The Mental Approach

Softball, like its companion sport, baseball, is as much a mental game as it is a physical game. For example, how well a player swings a bat, using all of the coordinated actions of the various body parts, depends upon how well that player learns the fundamentals of the great but often unfathomable art of hitting. Before a person can hit the ball properly, there must be a concentrated learning process where the mind is first introduced to and then accepts the correct principles. Only from that point can the player use correct body mechanics to become a good hitter...and that follows with every other aspect of the game—pitching, fielding and baserunning.

But before the start of long hours of instruction, practice and playing, a more important mental process must take place—enjoying the chance to play and taking every advantage to hit, catch and throw a ball. Softball is still a game, meant to be fun while providing an outlet for competitive instincts. A person must first mentally accept the game as such and want to play it; then the learning process and ultimately the chance to excel and gain a full measure of satisfaction will come.

The reasons why people want to play softball don't matter. For example, on the intercollegiate level, where I have coached for more than three decades, softball is the women's equivalent of men's baseball, and many, many schools throughout the country offer scholarships to outstanding female softball players. Even the schools that don't offer scholarships still have outstanding programs, because more and more girls are playing the sport in high school and in community leagues and have developed their skills to a point where they can compete at higher organized levels. Believe me, the competition in intercollegiate women's softball is just as intense as any I have seen in during my seasons of coaching baseball.

Many like the sport because it suits their physical skills. There are men who played baseball in their PeeWee League days but who found that their skills did not match up with others when they reached higher levels of competition. Rather than give up the idea of putting bat to ball, some play fast-pitch softball while others go on to slow-pitch softball. (A note of caution: playing fast-pitch softball is at least as fast and demanding a game as hardball, particularly when it comes to hitting. No one "moves down" to play it.)

Finally, age creates a lot of softball converts. Participants in slow-pitch can get just as much enjoyment for a much longer period of time without the rigorous performance that baseball and fast-pitch demands from their bodies. Softball will endure because even if bodies and skills deteriorate, minds still have a need to hit, catch, and throw a ball, and playing softball becomes a passion.

You Gotta Have Fun

Long before players get to the intense mental teaching/learning stage, they have first accepted the fun aspects of the game. It was then that they wanted to learn as much about softball as they could so they could improve and become as good as their skills allowed. The reason is simple: they discovered that the better they played, the more they enjoyed playing. Finding pleasure in something is the motor that drives anyone to become a constant participant, and it then propels the mind to seek new means to heighten the enjoyment.

All of this begins with the right mental approach, and that means primarily being willing to work as long and hard as possible to perfect skills. At the same time, you must form your own game plan as to how to proceed and then have the mental discipline to follow it. This need not be drudgery. Once the game becomes fun, then so should everything else that is associated with it. If you love to hit a ball, then you should enjoy all of the practice hours that go into hitting the ball. Let's face it, batting practice is the most fun you can have because hitting is probably what you enjoy most about the game. How can you lose? You really can't if you look on every hitting opportunity in practice as a way to improve your skills. But this also means total concentration to perfect all of the body movements that will make you a good hitter.

There Is Time to Learn—But Not to Think

In athletics, where individual instincts govern actions and reactions, the learning process must be so intensive that the mind really is little more than the explosive force that fires instantaneous thoughts into actions and reactions.

I once read something from a former major leaguer that struck me as being right on. He wrote that answering the challenge offered by opposing pitchers "was as much mental agility as it was physical ability." On the other hand, we all laughed when the inimitable Yogi Berra once asked, almost in desperation, "How can I hit and think at the same time?" The answer is of course that no one can do that if the ball is screaming toward the plate at ninety miles per hour.

However, if you work at the game and play it as much as possible, then the physical movements will be so automatic that you won't become frustrated by having to think, "Now what do I do?" There simply isn't time in either baseball or fast-pitch softball hitting to think of little more than "Do I want to hit this pitch?"

There certainly is a lot more to the game than the pitcher throwing the ball and the hitter striking it. The hours of mental preparation, abetted by physical practice, is an unseen force whose importance can be appreciated and understood only by those who have played the game. They know that playing the game demands a serious approach at becoming skilled and that a player must possess the necessary mental qualities to develop the proper techniques.

Have a Game Plan—Even When You Practice

There are four areas that must be perfected if you want to become a good hitter. Each day, in practice or in a game, you should concentrate fully on getting them right. The four areas follow.

1. *Learn the strike zone.* No one, regardless of the quality of their eyesight, will swing only at pitches in the strike zone. So you must be prepared and willing to go after a pitch that will be close to the strike zone. But if you don't concentrate on the limits of the strike zone, you will too often swing at bad pitches. Knowing the strike zone enables you to be selective in the choice of pitches and not be at the mercy of the pitcher who wants nibbles at bad pitches.

2. *Keep your eyes on the ball.* This takes absolute concentration—a stiff mental exercise. It is a necessary form of discipline to watch the ball from the moment it leaves the pitcher's hand until the instant you decide whether or not to swing. Too many hitting opportunities are wasted because hitters take their eyes from the ball. The only way you can hit a ball is to see it. The only way you can see it is to concentrate on looking at it.

3. *Learn to use the entire field.* Don't become so trapped by your hitting method that you can only hit to one area of the field. Learn how to hit the ball where it is pitched (by properly positioning the barrel of the bat to the ball), and how to handle the bat so that you don't get handcuffed by certain pitches. This, again, requires concentration and the desire to learn the necessary skills.

4. *Learn the proper hitting techniques.* I will lay out a "feel point" system in the next chapter that will be an easy guide for you to know whether or not you are following the proper principles for swinging the bat. But merely learning the principles is only one part of the game; it will take constant practice to hone your skills to a point where any deviation will ring an instant alarm. So the idea is first to learn and

then to perfect. Only then can you understand what Yogi Berra was talking about.

When in Doubt, Find Out

Hitters should never hesitate to ask for help from an instructor they trust. At the same time, they should not be jumping from instructor to instructor as if someone will finally give them a magic formula to make them instantaneous .300 hitters. This is particularly true for young players who may be impatient to become proficient at hitting a ball without bothering to realize that a good player isn't perfected in a day...or a week...or a month...or ever. Otherwise, every hitter would bat 1.000. As it is, hitting .300 is considered the benchmark of a good hitter. That means success in only three out of ten tries. Even good hitters must work on solving the problems from those other seven failures.

Here are some tips to follow:

1. *Keep an open mind.* Allow the coach time to prove that his or her methods can work with you, and do it by working to perfect all of the instruction the coach has provided. If that becomes impossible, or you simply disagree with the style you are learning, then be honest and tell the coach that some other instructor may be better suited to help you.

2. *Never kid yourself that you are "too tired" to work for improvement.* There will be times when your mind—and even your body—will try to convince you that fatigue really is too big an obstacle to overcome that day. Don't give in. Instead, develop a mental toughness so that no obstacle will ever keep you from improving every time you play. That will carry over in game situations so that your mind will never concede anything to a pitcher, regardless of his skill. Mental toughness builds confidence, and confidence is one main ingredient a successful hitter takes to the plate.

3. *Be willing to hit, and then hit some more.* You won't ever bat 1.000 for a season, but you certainly might become a consistent .300 hitter if you take every opportunity to practice your hitting. I've seen too many potentially good, young hitters get in some solid swings and then believe they have done enough for the day. There really is no such thing as "enough" hitting practice, and all you need do is look at the careers of the great hitters to know that they haunted batting cages, as well as pestered coaches and friends to throw more batting practice for them. Make it enjoyable for yourself away from the organized practice sessions and get your friends out for some

informal drills or pickup games where you can get more swings. Do it every day, if possible.

4. *Set some goals.* Give yourself something to shoot for, and then work until you attain it. And once attained, set another goal so that you constantly are pursuing a different result and are never satisfied with a single achievement. Make the goal reasonable, one that will reflect the results of your work and bring a measure of satisfaction. Often, young players set goals beyond their immediate reach and then get frustrated when they cannot attain them. Then they may begin to doubt their abilities and lose the necessary confidence they require to continue to improve.

5. *And you coaches* ... Use the old KISS method—Keep It Simple, Stupid. Don't bog down your pupils in technicalities so they are distracted or confused from the basic principles that they need to learn. Remember, all of those technical details may be good for conversation or debate with your peers, but a player doesn't have time to think about them at bat.

II. The Feel Point System

When I was the head baseball coach at the University of Northern Colorado several years ago, I was presented with an opportunity to teach baseball to hearing-impaired children. As you can guess, many of my conventional teaching methods had to be altered simply because these kids couldn't hear what I was saying and I did not know the sign language system well enough to make the necessary technical points about the mechanics of hitting.

I finally came up with a system I call the "See and Feel System of Hitting," or simply "feel points." Using feel points, these young players could recognize whether they were swinging the bat properly by the "feel" their body received from the almost instantaneous circuit of muscular reactions. It meant breaking down every body movement used in hitting and isolating the reactions—stretches or force against a surface or an object—that are involved. In the end, it was a made-to-order system.

I continued to develop the system because I believed that if it worked for kids with a disability, then it certainly would work for any other player. Also, since it was to be used primarily during practice, then it was something that players could do on their own.

Feel Points: How They Work

In the See and Feel System of Hitting, part of which we will cover in this chapter and part of which we'll cover elsewhere in the book, the individual can learn, through perfect practice, the following pointers:

1. How to establish a hitting posture by aligning the body parts into comfortable angles in the joint areas, with "feel points" to tell the hitter if the correct movements are being used during practice;

2. How to learn the five basic hitting movements and a feel point for each one, in correct sequence;

3. How to learn the specific movements that are isolated and practiced with a series of drills;

4. How to integrate specific movements through "sensory drills" for part of the hitting movement; and

5. How to use all of the hitting drills in a proper sequence.

This method will provide the hitter and a coach with a feedback system of sensory memory, rather than an oral or verbal memory, and create a retentive process for correctly practicing the hitting drills.

Feel Points: What They Are

A feel point is a muscular contraction stretch or force at a particular joint area during each segment of the skill movements when a player swings a bat. The areas are located in the muscles of the feet, ankles, knees, hips, shoulders, elbows, wrists and fingers. This book will show you the correct and comfortable way to stand at the plate and how to properly swing the bat. Then, if you learn the feel points, you will be able to recognize the precise muscular action that occurs at each of those areas when the hitting movements are executed. That precise sensation soon will become part of your brain's sensory memory, and whenever you swing a bat, the brain will telegraph a sensation as to whether or not the correct muscular contractions have occured.

For example, from constant repetition, a feel point hitter knows that certain muscular stretches or force occur at the forearms from the tightening or squeezing of the last three fingers of each hand as the bat is swung and contacts the ball. At this point, the brain records them for reference whenever the hitter is working on that particular area. Another area is a muscular stretch at the front shoulder area when the hitter coils the shoulders and arms inward prior to starting the swing. And a third instance occurs during the swing as the rear foot pushes against the ground as it pivots to turn the rear vertical half of the body.

How will you be able to know all of this has occurred? There is a three-fold progression: see it, touch it, feel it from within.

Setting Up the Hitting Posture

Before you can even begin to swing a bat, you must be standing in the correct hitting posture. The lower and upper half of the body each have three feel points for identifying the correct position.

BOTTOM HALF HITTING POSTURE

Establish a balanced hitting stance for the stride and rear foot/hip acceleration process by spreading the feet as wide as possible. When you turn the rear foot/hip at this wide stance you'll find it is slow.

Keep moving the rear foot forward to shorten the distance until you finally find a comfortable position to allow the rear foot and hip to turn quickly as a unit. This will accelerate the power of the swing. Once you have established your foot position, mark the spots for each foot on the ground. They become your "stride marks."

Place another mark between the two marks. Once the stride is completed and the rear foot/hip has turned, the front of the rear knee should be approximately in straight line to that new mark. If the rear knee is beyond the middle mark, you have lunged and lost the rear hip acceleration. If that is the case, bring the front foot six to eight inches toward the rear foot.

• *Feel Point 1 (Knee Angles):* Bend a little at the waist toward the inside of the plate, and bend both knees slightly as well. Feel the action of *muscular contraction at the top of the knees.* That slight angle in the knees, particularly in the rear leg, is important because it exerts force against the ground to power the rear pivot foot.

• *Feel Point 2 (Vertical Balance): Lift the toes of both feet and feel the pressure on the inside portion of the big toes and inside the heels of both feet.* Once the feel points for the feet are recognized, the toes can return to the ground and relax. This feel point establishes a vertical body balance with a slight horizontal move for the hitting movements.

• *Feel Point 3 (Incline Rear Knee):* Move the rear knee toward the inside of the front knee while maintaining the rear knee angle. This automatically *increases the pressure, or force, from the inside ball of the foot* against the ground for the rear foot pivot movement.

UPPER HALF HITTING POSTURE

• *Feel Point 4 (Grip Pressure):* The bat should rest in the fingers not in the palm. Using a split knuckles alignment for the grip, *be sure the fingers are firm but relaxed.* The second set of knuckles of the top hand should split the second and third sets of knuckles of the bottom hand.

• *Feel Point 5 (Bat Placement):* Place the bat and hands at the ready position at the shoulder and *extend the thumb of the top hand so that it touches the outer edge of the rear shoulder,* creating a proper ninety-degree angle by the front arm at the elbow joint.

• *Feel Point 6 (Shoulder Coil):* Raise the bat slightly and coil the shoulder so that the arms and the shoulders are positioned slightly inward. You will *feel a minor muscular contraction on the inside of the front shoulder and a muscular stretch at the outer part of the front shoulder.* The position of the rear elbow is an individual preference. You may have it up with the arm parallel to the ground, or you may have it facing downward at approximately forty-five degrees. Check the proper downward angle and position of the elbow in front of a mirror.

With those six basic points, you can perfect the establishment of your pre-hitting position.

The Hitting Movements

Now that you have your hitting posture, you're ready to swing. There are five basic hitting movements. Each is accompanied by a specific feel point to help you recognize the movement.

1. *The Stride.* This is a slow, short, soft plant of the foot on a forty-five-degree angle.

• *Feel Point 7:* The feel point for the stride is the *pressure felt along the total inner edge of the front foot* when it is positioned at a forty-five-degree angle.

2. *Pull/Push of Arms.* Both arms start forward together. With the grip intact, bottom hand moves downward so the back of the hand and the top of the forearm face upward, and the palm of the bottom hand faces down. This process is called pronation. At the same time, the top hand will perform a motion called supination, which is the rotation of the forearm and hand backward and away from the body's midline, and the direction of the palm of the hand upward. This moves the bat forward—by way of a small arc from the outer edge of the shoulder—and into the path of the ball.

• *Feel Point 8:* As the hands are in their pronation-supination mode, *the top hand slightly pushes against the bottom hand whose thumb side turns down.*

3. *Arm Extension* and 4. *Rear Foot Pivot.* We must link these two together. The latter is a slight pivot with the rear foot, which turns the back hip and forces the edge of the big toes of the front foot against the ground. At the same time, the rear elbow moves slightly down and diagonally away from the hip and the stomach area, as the arms begin to fully extend, again guiding the bat into the path of the ball. That movement causes the last three fingers of each hand to tighten as the bat contacts the ball. The two movements will be complete as the rear foot pivots at the snap of both arms.

• *Feel Point 9: There will be a muscular contraction felt in the forearms from the fingers squeezing the bat.*

• *Feel Point 10: You can feel the inside of the big toe of the rear foot as it pushes against the ground.* There can be a full pivot for an inside pitch or a quarter turn for an outside pitch.

5. *Follow-Through.* After the bat makes contact with the ball, the top hand will "roll over" the bottom hand to ensure that the swing makes a full arc and that the bottom arm collapsing at the elbow toward the waist does not cut short the swing. You should make sure to keep the bat at a forty-five-degree angle facing upward or the barrel may swing too low (finishing at the middle of your back). Your body may thrust forward slightly at the contact of the ball, also causing a slight forward weight transfer. The turn need not be drastic because that can throw the body out of line and cost it power from the rear foot pivot in movement 4.

• *Feel Point 11: These are muscular stretches felt at the rear shoulder and rear upper arm, and inside the top of the thigh in the front leg or atop the leg just below the waist.* The knee of the front leg points at a forty-five-degree angle, and the rear foot points toward the pitcher.

How to Use Those Feel Points

Now that you know the feel points, you can use them, along with a full-length mirror, to record sensory and visual images of your correct swing. Once accomplished, you never again will have to wonder whether you are doing it correctly. An imprecise move will be telegraphed by an imprecise muscular contraction.

The feel points help in the two crucial areas of hitting. They can be used to get set in the *hitting posture*, and they can be used for the five hitting movements to create the perfect swing. Remember, the most important thing is to know when you are in a correct and balanced position and to coordinate the top and bottom halves of your body.

III. Selecting a Bat

The most prized possession of every good hitter is the bat. We've all heard tales of players sleeping with their bats in good times, and sawing them up during batting slumps (now a bit hard with the proliferation of aluminum bats). Good hitters are almost never without their bats. They swing them in front of mirrors and in the emptiness of open fields, they cradle them while sitting on the bench between innings, and they rant and rave if someone else uses them.

Selecting your bat is the one thing over which you should strive to have total control. Do it the same way you purchase your clothes, and use the same considerations. When buying clothes, you insist that they fit, and you want them to feel just right and allow you the freedom to move as you wish. Selecting a bat is no different, only in this case let your hands do the talking. And unlike clothes buying, don't be too influenced by the brand name on the bat barrel.

I know that many who play on teams in leagues and schools have a bunch of bats available—and it is understood that all of our discussions here revolve primarily around the use of aluminum bats, which are so predominant at every level of play—that someone may have purchased for the general use. This is very helpful, but go beyond that if possible, and get your own bats—it's only a modest investment, and there is no price that can be placed on the positive psychological effects that using the right bat will provide.

For one thing, you simply feel good walking up to the plate knowing that you have a stick with which you feel comfortable. Can you imagine what that alone will do for your confidence level? It has to mean something because we all have read countless stories of major league hitters and some of the traumas that they undergo when they cannot get a bat that suits them. Sometimes they'll rummage through the bat bag and come up with one that feels just right, and a teammate may be missing a bat or two for a while. Or players have gone into mental funks because they ran out of bats and were awaiting a resupply from a dealer. In the meantime, as they scrambled to try and succeed with a borrowed bat, a black cloud seemed to hover over their head and their batting.

What are the consequences of not using a comfortable bat? Call upon your own experience and you may remember taking one up to the plate that is too heavy, too light, too long, or too short, and you wind up thinking to yourself, "Gee I *hope* this will be okay."

Hope is not what you want when you go to bat, and if that is all you can muster then mark yourself down as indecisive...and probably out.

Be Picky When Picking Out a Bat

As I noted, selecting a bat is like buying new clothes—your preference, please. Here are some of the keys:

1. *Select one that feels comfortable.* Be sure that it fits the hands. When selecting a bat, what does it feel like as it nestles atop the fingers? People with small hands often don't want a fat-handled bat because they really can never get a comfortable grip. Instead, they need a thinner handle. So will many power hitters because it will be quicker going around and quicker in their hands. Conversely, players with large hands may not feel comfortable using a thin-handled bat because there simply is not enough to grasp. That is where measuring for comfort is important. They may have to settle for a larger handled bat with a bigger barrel.

2. *Weight distribution.* A strong, quick hitter will want more weight toward the end of the bat. A hitter who works to place the ball to all fields will want to use as much of the bat as possible and should seek a bat whose weight is equally distributed along the barrel. However, when you choose your bat don't get caught up in the bat speed, because the bat doesn't supply the speed, the batter supplies it. The problem arises if you're swinging a bat that is too heavy and simply overpowers some of your natural bat speed. The main thing is to get a bat that feels comfortable and can be easily handled. How do you know? Again, like clothes buying, it isn't a bad idea to try many before deciding which feels best.

Note: In *slow-pitch softball*, where there is time to track a ball and draw a good bead on it, many hitters prefer the big power swing, so they look for a heavier bat. In *fast-pitch softball*, hitters don't worry as much about the weight but about having a bat that allows them to make contact more easily, because the pitcher will supply the power just from the velocity of his pitches. In all cases where there is indecision, you should go with the lighter bat because it will not impede your swing as much as the heavier models.

Be Certain the Bat's Shape Fits You

Bats come in a variety of shapes, and all are manufactured to suit the varied needs of all kinds of hitters, as well as to cater to their physical size and how they feel comfortable using it at the plate. Let's look at the most common:

1. *A thin-handled bat with more weight on the end.* Many power hitters prefer this kind of bat because they can produce greater speed and velocity, and that big head at the end can often explode the ball into the far reaches of an outfield where it will not be caught.

However, if the hitter who selects a bat with too much weight on the end is not strong and has small hands—this is a problem that young players and some female hitters must face—he or she will have problems handling the bat. It is better for hitters in this group to seek a bat where the weight is equally distributed.

2. *Bats with big barrels.* Many power hitters believe the bigger barrel provides them with more hitting surface. Power hitters also can get bigger barrelled bats without thin handles but with adequate weight distribution—those with big hands should consider this type—and still produce power.

3. *Equally distributed weight.* Many hitters prefer a bat where the weight is equal up and down the barrel because they feel they will have greater bat control. This is particularly apt for fast-pitch softball where hitters don't have time for the big swing, and many players are more comfortable with the feeling of shortening their swing. Also in this group are hitters who are not particularly strong and who rely on bat control to spray the ball.

It's Not the Length—It's the Comfort

A bat's length need not be a problem but it can vary. Basically, some long-armed hitters like to use a longer bat because they feel they get more leverage. This can range to the 32-34 inch size, with a weight of 25-28 ounces. Young players can use bats of 31 to 33 inches (we're still talking about aluminum bats) and around 30 ounces. Again the key is to try several bats in synch with your arm length and see which feels comfortable. Certainly, if you have long arms a 32-inch bat will feel strange from the moment you pick it up. Your body will know as you go through the testing stage, and then so will you.

A good rule of thumb for those who don't have a bat of their own and must feed out of the bat rack: if the available bats don't feel comfortable, then find the one that comes closest and choke up on it at the plate. If possible, bring it further back toward the rear shoulder to regain the comfort feeling.

IV. The Stance

Fast-Pitch Softball

If you think it is difficult to hit a baseball, then sometime try hitting against a great fast-pitch softball pitcher.

Many believe that the larger sized softball should be easier to hit than a baseball, but the shorter distance between the pitcher's mound and home plate plus the pitcher's speed—to say nothing of the way in which a pitcher can make the ball rise and fall or slip and slide—negates any advantage of going after a bigger target.

That is why hitting techniques must be precise and polished. There is a premium on solid fundamentals, which become good habits, as well as split-second decision making. A fault in any of the elements that are part of the hitting technique can handicap a hitter to the point of desperation.

All that we will cover in the next few chapters will eventually lead up to the proper way to hit a softball in the fast-pitch game.

The Fundamentals of the Stance

How a batter stands in the box—the stance—becomes a player's trademark. Most of us have seen a myriad of stances by great major league hitters, each different, some oddly so, yet all are effective for that particular player. Hence, it is not how you stand that makes the difference so much as what you do while you are standing there.

Nonetheless, there are certain fundamentals that are important to follow when you're setting up a proper stance. One of the most important is the distance between the feet. Add to this the distance you select to the inside edge of the plate, and you have a stride base for initiating and generating power from the rear foot. As we shall see, the force generated from the inside ball of the rear foot and big toe accelerates the rear hip and rear shoulder, which in turn transmits power to the shoulders as they coordinate with the extended arms that are propelling the bat.

Therefore, there are three major functions of your stance:

1. Support for the body;

FIGURE 4-1

ACHIEVING BALANCE WITH TOE CURLS: *To get the correct balance in the stance, curl the toes upward (4-1), and feel the pressure along the inside of the balls of the feet and heels. Drop down toes and you'll naturally assume a good, balanced stance.*

2. Body balance, before, during and after the swing; and

3. Maintenance of angles in the knees to facilitate the linear (stepping into pitch, weight transfer) and rotary (hips opening) movements.

How you use them is also a major consideration. Here are some basic considerations:

1. Be certain that the undersides of your athletic shoes are clean and that they hug the surface of the ground without any discomfort. That will help you get a secure and firm foot position.

2. Check to see that the ground in the box is even so you will have a comfortable platform under your feet. If you are not on a level platform, or one that fits your particular stance, then you won't have a comfortable swing.

3. Don't rush into the batter's box. Take enough time so that you can be as comfortable as possible. Don't allow the pitcher or catcher, or even the umpire, to hurry you to the point where you won't set up comfortably with your hitting posture and establish plate coverage.

4. Don't stand too close or too far from the plate. Be certain to measure the entire area with your bat by extending the bat with the bottom hand and touching the outside of the plate. You'll know you can get anything in the strike zone and that any ball that comes over the plate is yours if you wish to swing. That is a confidence booster.

How Wide Is the Stance?

There is no such thing as a "proper" foot width. Young players should stand so they can comfortably swing without striding too far with the front foot. They shouldn't be spread so far that they get little acceleration from their rear foot/hip for the swing.

Stand in front of a mirror and check your stance. Does it look comfortable? Better still, does it feel comfortable? Have you incorporated the first three feel points? Decide for yourself whether it feels natural and comfortable, and then take a couple of swings to see if it looks as comfortable as it may feel. Do that until you are satisfied that you have a stance that will fit your dimensions, and then lock it into your memory bank. If you get into a slump, you can return to that mirror and rerun a mental movie of the time when you were pleased with your stance.

We've all heard a so-called "rule of thumb" that says the stance or spread of the feet should be no wider than the shoulders. While spreading the feet to shoulder width is a good starting point, it is *not* a hard and fast rule. To the contrary, a wide stance can get a hitter in trouble because it can inhibit the desired acceleration process of the rear hip. The wide base also decreases the angle of the rear knee, and the upper and lower leg on the ground, further diminishing the acceleration of the rear hip. Take too long a stride and the entire body will move, including the eyes from the path of the ball. Gone will be the ability to get a solid hit.

At the same time, don't make the stance too narrow. This causes an unstable and out of balance feeling while swinging, creating a lunging effect with the body weight moving toward the ball. You may find yourself a bit out of control and a ready victim for a good change of speed pitcher.

You must feel comfortable with the spread of the feet and be able to transfer the body weight from the rear foot to the braced front foot, without disturbing the equal weight distribution between the two. The best way to achieve this is to start with a *parallel or square/straight-away stance*. The feet should be comfortably set, as we noted, with the toes on a straight line parallel to the inside line of the batter's box.

FIGURE 4-2A

FIGURE 4-2B

FIGURE 4-2C

STANCES: *The open stance (4-2A) aligns the front foot away from the plate. The closed stance (4-2B) positions the front foot closer to the plate. The square or parallel stance (4-2C) shows both feet parallel to the inside line of the batter's box.*

The front foot should bisect an imaginary line through the middle of home plate. The stance can be toward the front of the box, back, inside or away, depending on your strengths and the pitcher's.

For hitters who are extremely quick in reacting to the ball and particularly strong in the upper half of the body, a *closed stance* is sometimes effective. If this seems good for you, your front foot will be closer to the plate and pointed toward the opposite field, somewhat forward of an imaginary line drawn from the toes of the back foot to the pitcher. This prevents your front side from opening too quickly, which in turn can pull the front shoulder and front hip off the ball prior to the swing.

The *open stance* is often effective for the hitter who is slower to move the front hip to an open position, but this stance leaves the hitter vulnerable to outside pitches. The front foot is pointed away from the center of the field at an approximate forty-five-degree angle to an imaginary line, slightly toward the foul line.

Positioning the Feet

All the power produced in the swing begins, as we noted, with the rear foot. So plant that foot firmly when you take your stance, even if

FIGURE 4-3

WRAPPED BAT POSITON:
*Starting with the bat in a 45°
plane, move the barrel further to
the rear feeling stretch along front
of upper front arm (Feel Point #6).
This position can increase bat
speed for players with extra
strong forearms, wrists and
hands.*

PLATE COVERAGE: *A check of plate coverage should be made at the ready position of the stance, as shown, and after a normal stride. All of the strike zone must be reachable.*

FIGURE 4-4

you must dig a small hole. That gives you something from which to push forward. Even after the weight transfer takes place from back to front, that rear foot will be firmly planted to provide the necessary balance for the follow-through.

While we will discuss the stride in an upcoming chapter, you must coordinate your foot position with the length of your stride. Consider a stride of eight inches or less, because the shorter the stride, the better balance you'll maintain, and that will keep your head and eyes in place to track the pitch.

In fast-pitch, don't stride in different directions to hit various types of pitches, even if you are trying to hit the ball to the opposite field. Instead, move *both feet* to a different position prior to the pitch being delivered. Moving just one foot can throw off the stride. Slow-pitch offers other alternatives, but this is discussed in a later chapter.

Faults

1. *Stance too narrow.* Causes overstriding and losing sight of the pitch.

2. *Stance too wide.* Causes the hips to lock and decreases the power and proper weight transfer from the rear foot to the front foot through the rear hip.

3. *Rear foot pointing away from the pitcher.* Prevents a weight shift, rear hip turn and proper turn of the rear foot.

4. *Weight on balls of feet.* Proper balance isn't established, causing a forward lean toward the plate prior to hitting the ball; makes it hard to hit an inside pitch.

5. *Weight on heels of feet.* Causes you to move away from the ball and loss of balance.

6. *Standing too far from the plate.* You are unable to cover the entire strike zone and many pitches hit off the end of the bat.

7. *Standing too close to the plate.* Most pitches are hit off the bat handle; also inhibits full arm extension.

8. *Weight not transferred from rear to front leg at ball contact.* Weight remains on the back foot despite a rear foot pivot.

V. Gripping the Bat

A good swing begins with the way in which the bat is held. There are some who advocate a pressure grip, one that seems almost to squeeze out what life there is in that stick, but nothing could be worse. Instead, be nice...be gentle but firm...and always be in control.

It may sound simple but often hitting problems can begin with an improper grip. To alleviate that dire potential, here is a good routine to follow.

Place the bat in the hands so that it crosses the crease where the fingers attach to the palm of the hands. In reality, you are holding the bat on the fingers and away from the palm of the hand. Never hold it deep in the palm because most hitters—probably about ninety-five percent—do not have hands thick enough to provide a cushion from the recoil that occurs when the bat strikes the ball. If it hits the bone area between the thumb and forefinger, a batter's hands can become so sore that it may be impossible to grip a bat for several days. Holding it closer to the fingers provides the necessary space to absorb the recoil. As far as I know, the only exception to this rule was Harmon Killebrew, the great Hall of Fame hitter from the Minnesota Twins who hit over 500 home runs during his major league career. But Harmon's hands were unusual in that they were thick, with not particularly graceful fingers, and it was uncomfortable for him to lay the bat in his fingertips and try to grip it.

The grip is slightly different for each hand. In the bottom hand, the bat is placed across the pads of the palm. When the fingers close around the bat, they secure the bat in the part of the palm closest to the fingers, and furthest from the thumb. In the top hand, the initial placement is similar but upon the closing of the hand the bat is firmly in the grip of fingers and padding of the palm—right in the crease where the fingers attach to the palm of the hand. The top hand, which controls the swing, must be able to accurately direct the bat, and this cannot be done if the bat is deep in the palm.

Once you are comfortable with the bat in your fingertips, close the fingers around the handle of the bat, and it will feel relaxed in the pads of both hands. The second knuckle of the top hand should be lined up with the third knuckle of the lower hand, and the third knuckle of the top hand should be in line with the second knuckle of the bottom hand. Next, give the top hand a quarter turn clockwise so the

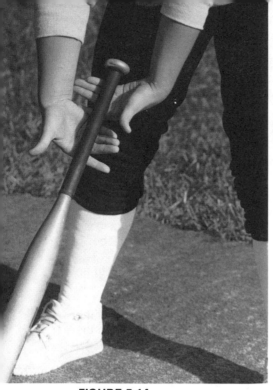

FIGURE 5-1A

FIGURE 5-1B

FIGURE 5-1C

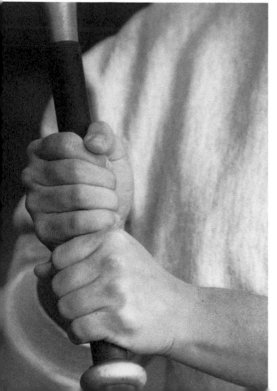

GRIPPING THAT BAT: *The bat should be gripped across the finger pads and fingers of the hands. Avoid putting the bat deep into the palms (5-1A). Lift the bat to shoulder level (5-1B) and then turn the top hand so that the second set of knuckles of the top hand dissects the second and third sets of knuckles of the bottom hand (5-1C).*

middle knuckle splits the second and third knuckles of the bottom hand. This alignment aids in the positioning of the hand, the forearms, and the bat for proper extension when you swing.

Allow the second, third and little fingers of both hands, with the first finger and each thumb lending lesser support, to hold the bat firmly but relaxed against the pads of each hand, in the ready position. If you squeeze the bat in this position its movement will be slower. But if you allow the fingers and hands to firm up automatically at the moment of contact, any prior movement with the bat will not be inhibited, an action that is similar to tightening the grip on the steering wheel of a car when making a quick turn.

Be certain that both hands are four to five inches in front of you and aligned with your rear foot and knee and about three or four inches to the rear of your back knee.

Holding the Bat In the Ready Position

One of the simplest ways to position the bat and hands at the ready position is to bring the bat up to the shoulder and extend the thumb of the top hand so that it touches the outer edge of the rear shoulder. This is feel point 5, described in Chapter II.

Notice the ninety-degree angle that is created by the front arm at the elbow joint. It is important to maintain that ninety-degree angle because it creates acceleration at the elbow joint to drive the forearm and hands into the proper extension. The movement is similar to a karate chop.

The rear elbow should point downward at approximately a forty-five-degree angle, about six to eight inches away from the rear side of the body. The muscular stretch on the outside of the front shoulder and the contraction on the inside are feel point 6.

Three Positions of the Bat

The bat can be positioned in three ways prior to initiating the swing. The first is a *vertical position,* which gives the hitter a feeling of having little or no weight in the hands. Some use this to initiate quicker bat movement to the swing position. A *forty-five-degree angle* can be achieved by moving the hands toward the rear shoulder. The thumb side of the bottom hand must turn downward to create the palm down/palm up effect. Finally, the *flat position* brings the barrel of the bat directly into the path of the ball.

FIGURE 5-2A
FIGURE 5-2C

FIGURE 5-2B

BAT POSITIONS: *The vertical position (5-2A), the bat held straight up and down, gives the hitter a feeling of weightlessness until launch. Batters most commonly position the bat at a 45° angle (5-2B). The flat, or horizontal, position (5-2C) gets the bat into the path of the oncoming pitch faster but presents problems when hitting high pitches (swinging under the pitch).*

Choking Up for Bat Control

There are players in fast-pitch competition who may need to shorten their swing to better cope with the speed of the pitches. Let me say at the outset that this is not a sign of weakness nor will it rob you of your power. Too often, hitters get caught up with the notion of not conceding anything to the pitcher, to the point of being stubbornly foolish. The pitcher is looking for any edge possible, and you will play right into that pitcher's hands. Don't be afraid to choke up from the very first time you begin taking batting practice, and continue it during a game.

Coming up the handle a half inch or even an inch gives you a better chance to get the best part of the bat on the ball. It will also give you more confidence that you can cope with any pitch, and with that confidence will come consistent production...and yes, even power. Don't wait for two strikes to come up on the bat, either. You may have already wasted a couple of solid hitting opportunities.

Here's another tip. Many major league players will mark with a piece of tape the spot on the bat where they feel most comfortable choking up. It is a quick, handy, fail-safe reference point.

Obviously, hitters without much power, who rely on bat control for

FIGURE 5-3

CHOKING THE BAT: *Choking the bat will provide better control and a quicker bat (because the weight of the barrel is closer to the hands and easier to propel).*

their hits, should choke up because this gives them added ability to control the bat's weight and guide the ball to different fields. But line drive and home run hitters should also be willing to come up the bat when necessary. Power hitters, particularly, often are sensitive about this, but if they hit consistently with power, they won't lose any coming up a half inch or even an inch up from the knob. With better bat control, they will do it more consistently.

Consider these points about choking up:

1. It will help your concentration, whether you are a power hitter or one who survives by spraying the ball;

2. You will have better balance and an opportunity to hit the ball on the best part of the bat;

3. You get a shorter, more compact swing because the bat has less distance to travel, which will help your concentration, particularly if you have two strikes;

4. You'll produce more line drives and have better bat control to hit to the open areas of the field; and

5. Choking up provides better bat control, and it means not getting jammed as much from inside pitches. You can turn those pitches into base hits instead of foul balls or ineffective infield dribblers.

VI. How to Use the Hands

The first commandment to the proper use of the hands in hitting is very simple:

Don't take them for granted.

The second commandment is just as simple:

Use both of them every time you swing a bat...and for as long as the bat is being swung.

Every hitting instructor at every level of competition during the past several years has been faced with the problem of teaching young—and not so young—hitters that the practice of releasing the top hand from the bat before the swing is completed is not necessarily going to make them good hitters, even though this is used by a few major league stars. Much of this is the result of the so-called Charley Lau school of hitting, which has been popularized by George Brett and Wade Boggs. It began as a teaching point to emphasize a strong extension and prohibit the top hand from rolling over the bottom hand prior to or during contact with the ball.

Unfortunately, the inexperienced hitter may relax the grip, particularly the top hand, too quickly after contact and therefore lose the acceleration of the bat after it hits the ball. In a general sense, every hitter will have a better opportunity to succeed if both hands stay on the bat until the entire follow-through process is completed. We'll look at this point in greater detail later in this chapter, but just remember one thing. How a batter uses the hands during his swing will determine just how successfully and frequently the base hits will come and how consistently the balls will be driven beyond the infield.

Position of the Hands

The hands serve an important function in hitting a ball. When used correctly, they move the bat barrel to a position of contact with the ball. Too often some hitting coaches say "Throw your hands at the ball." Nothing could be worse. When you relinquish control of your hands, you give up the opportunity to bring the bat into a direct and powerful line with the ball.

Actually, as we noted earlier in the book, the entire surfaces of the hands really do not come in full contact with the bat. Rather, the last three fingers of each hand are the keys as they squeeze and contract the muscles in various parts of the arms to create resistance to the ball while the barrel is accelerating through it.

Each hand plays a specific role in hitting. The bottom hand pulls the bat through the swing, and the top hand provides the bat speed while keeping the bat in control and balanced. They only are effective when working together, and when they aren't you will find out in a hurry—the hits will stop coming.

Here is an exercise that will help. Spread your hands on the bat, then swing it and feel how the front arm pulls and the rear arm pushes. Do each hand separately, then simultaneously.

There are some sound rules for positioning the hands. Keep the hands four to six inches from the body, comfortably set slightly beyond the back knee and slightly raised to form a coil three or four inches from the rear shoulder. The front elbow should be slightly down and close to the mid-chest level. The exact placement can be an individual preference, but it never should be so outlandish as to have the end of the bat above the ear or near the belt level. Just keep in mind that a properly positioned bat at the outset of a swing will make it more effective.

FIGURE 6-1A

PRONATION/SUPINATION (PALM DOWN/PALM UP) DRILL: *In 6-1A, the batter, while kneeling on the rear leg and grasping the front side at the waist with the top hand, swings the bat with the bottom hand (palm down, or in the pronation position). The follow-through should bring the bat around to a high finish. In 6-1B, the batter, while kneeling on the front leg and grasping the rear side at the waist with the bottom hand, swings the bat with top hand (palm up, or in the supination position). In 6-1C, the batter grips the bat with both hands and swings.*

FIGURE 6-1B

FIGURE 6-1C

Occasionally hitters—and everyone who ever has swung a bat probably has done it at one time or another—start with their hands in good position but reach up to eye level or higher to stroke a ball. It might be a bad pitch, but since the hands were properly set, the speed of the action was probably sufficient to hit those pitches.

But if you drop the hands too low *before* the pitch, then the swing becomes more complicated—and usually less effective. You must first bring the bat back up and into proper position before even beginning the swing. In fast-pitch softball, there is very little time to do anything but propel the bat forward, and hitters who must "reload" are asking to whiff.

Keeping the hands raised toward the outer edge of the shoulder means one less motion to worry about over microseconds when there is no time for any mental exercises. Remember, the less extra motion during the swing, the less room for a mistake.

How the hands are positioned on the bat is determined to a great extent by the split of the knuckles. They position the barrel of the bat to a direct path to the ball and transfer power from the rear leg, shoulders, arms and hand to the bat and into the ball. If the knuckles are in the proper position, the top hand twists slightly, pushing the bottom hand downward and forward, as both arms are extending. The palm of the bottom hand is then facing downward, and the top hand is in a palm-up position, guiding the barrel of the bat in a straight and powerful path to the ball.

Quiet Hands Speak Loudest

The term "quiet hands" means keeping the hands in place once the pitcher brings the arm around to release the ball. All of us have seen hitters at the plate twitching around to some extent, clasping and unclasping their hands from the bat handle. Those motions are acceptable when you begin to focus on the next pitch prior to it being released by the pitcher; it might be a way to build up the proper energy to swing. But any extreme movement of the hands after that really is a lack of discipline. A hitter with too much hand movement while the ball is en route to the plate will not have time to get ready to hit it. Everything will start too late, instead of already being locked into position where all that remains is to begin striding into the ball. If you are moving, the time it will take to stop and get locked into position will be consumed by the flight of the ball to the plate, and at best, all you can hope for is a halfway swing—and halfway results.

Does the Wrist Really Snap?

All of us have heard about "snapping the wrist" as being so important to good hitting. This is probably the most overblown bit of advice any hitters can get because there is no such thing as consciously snapping the wrist. All a hitter need do is to accelerate the extension of the bat and that so-called snap—really a natural slight twist of the hands just prior to contact with the ball continuing during the completion of the swing at the extension—will take care of itself. This occurs because of the alignment of the knuckles, which will position the top hand in a palm-up position.

But hitters never should consciously try to snap the wrist because they are in graver danger of short-stopping their full swing, with the resulting loss of power.

There are times when the wrist action can be important, but it is only when working with a fast bat and the forearms in a connected position. This will allow you to wait until the last possible moment to get after a pitch with some power.

Strong hands and wrists are something that can be physically developed by specific exercises. Use a rubber ball or a hand squeezer while sitting in front of the TV or walking or driving to build up hand strength. Tie a fifteen-pound weight at the end of a rope that reaches from your midsection to the ground and attach it to the center of a pole. While fully extending the arms parallel to the ground, wind the rope around the pole while rotating your wrists. Start this with three sets of five repetitions and work to three sets of twenty-five repetitions.

Beware the Slow Bat

The term "fast bat" was just mentioned above, and every hitter must work endlessly to maintain that action. The opposite, of course, is a slow bat, and that occurs from "slow hands" or when the two hands do not work in concert. The top hand is not moving fast enough to drive the bat because the bottom hand and arm are dominating the swing. You wind up missing pitches that you normally handle or, at best, you do not hit the ball hard. Hitters can notice the difference pretty quickly because they aren't handling mediocre pitches on the outside corner of the plate or they're themselves getting jammed by inside pitches.

Curing a "slow bat" is best done by taking as much extra hitting as possible and consciously getting back into good habits while swinging. Nothing cures problems like extra practice. You should also concentrate on getting better extension with the bat. There are some other adjustments that help, too: choking up on the bat, using a lighter one, shortening the swing by moving the bat closer to the outer edge of the shoulder, moving the bat slightly between the shoulder and the side of the head, or moving the body closer to the plate. You should also focus on pushing down hard and pivoting the rear foot, thus accelerate the opening of the hips.

Pepper is a good game to help speed up your bat. You must be quick with the bat in this game in order to keep the ball in play. And if all else fails—and long before that happens—constantly remind yourself, "I must be quick! I must be quick!"

VII. Striding to Hit

A great hitter once wrote, "Good hitting begins with the lower part of the body, and hitters who do not work hard to achieve sound, fundamental action down there will not do much with their bat."

The man had it all figured out.

You can figure it out, too. Try to swing a bat as if you are going to hit a ball. Without even thinking, you had to move your front foot because it was the most natural action a hitter can perform. Consider the alternative. Stand still without moving and try to swing. What happens? Not very much, certainly nothing that will allow you to hit a ball with any effectiveness.

A proper stride allows you to move the segments of the hitting movements in a perfectly balanced way. In so doing, you lessen your chances of being fooled by a pitch. You are in complete control of the plate at all times.

FIGURE 7-1

DEAD FOOT STRIDE PIVOT DRILL: *After assuming stance, stride with the front foot, being careful not to transfer any weight. Then push down on the ball of rear foot and rotate hips, while maintaining the 45° angle created by the front leg and upper body. This drill will help overcome the tendencies to lunge, overstride and/or prematurely open the hips.*

There are three different types of strides, but only one—the straight dead foot plant—is recommended for fast-pitch softball. The other two are good for the slow-pitch game. In the first, you lift your front knee and foot slightly in a straight line off the ground while planting the other foot firmly in place. In the second, you coil the front knee to link the plant foot while setting the rear foot slightly inward to create force at the ball of the foot. We will discuss these two actions in greater detail later in the book when we touch on slow-pitch hitting. For now, we will focus on the straight dead foot plant.

The "dead foot" really is the front or lead foot, and it is moved in a direct line toward the pitcher, keeping the toes as close as possible on a forty-five-degree angle, facing an imaginary line from the plate to the pitcher. When the dead foot plant is completed, a slight knee angle should be maintained. If you turn the toes too quickly toward the pitcher, the hips will open too soon. The key here is that only the front foot will move. Plant that rear foot and keep it firmly planted, with the slight knee angle, during this action because it will supply the power for turning the rear half of the body. That will happen if you push the inside of the ball of the rear foot against the ground, accelerating the opening of the hips in a proper sequence during the swing.

Don't Overstride

A hitter doesn't get power with a big stride. In fact it's just the opposite in most cases. We've all seen small players jerk a ball out of sight, and it seems as if they barely move toward their front foot when they swing. In reality, the "big striders" will lose power to accelerate the bat if their weight is spread too far between the feet.

How far is enough?

As we discussed in Chapter II, you should find out for yourself, first by spreading your legs as far as possible and then working the rear foot forward until there is a comfortable stance; six to eight inches is usually a good width. Soon, the body will memorize that particular action. Anything more or less will set off an alarm and you'll know there is a problem of overstriding or understriding. An overstride may bring the hands forward rather than keeping them back and ready to move the bat. If the overstride occurs with too much distance between the feet, the rear half pivoting process will suffer. When the hands come forward during a long stride, all you get is a slow, weak swing.

A more manageable movement will allow you to stay balanced, begin the hip action, and keep the swing in good rhythm. It also will allow you to keep your hips closed until you commit to a swing. If the front foot moves too far toward the plate during the stride, the hips will close further, and because of the larger stride, the shoulder and elbows will drop. That makes it difficult for the hands and bat to get into the hitting area, particularly if the pitch is on the inside of the strike zone.

However, if you stand further from the plate and stride to a closed stance position, then it is possible to hit the inside pitch, though the full rotary movement of the hips will be diminished. If your front foot moves too far from the plate (stepping in the bucket), your body will move slightly upward with your head and eyes following. This will open the hips too soon, making it difficult to hit a pitch from the middle of the plate, particularly an outside pitch. It will also give you a rather weak swing and a loss of power.

Keep one good rule in mind: the shorter the stride the better. Move the dead foot slightly into the stride position on the inside, and the big toe will strike the ground first at a forty-five-degree angle. But you also must be certain that the inside of the heel hits the ground without the body weight moving forward. The front knee should be slightly angled and braced. Too often a hitter will put the inside of the foot down and forget to put the heel down. If that happens, during the swinging action, the knee snaps back prior to the contact of the ball, leaving the weight on the rear foot without any rear hip rotary acceleration and weight transfer. You should "feel" the inner edge of your foot to be certain you have done it correctly. This is feel point 7.

Quiet Please, Front Foot

I'm certain you've heard the term "quiet foot" when hitting is discussed. It means that a proper striding technique with the front foot is nothing more than a gliding movement just above the ground. As we noted earlier, the front knee lift and the coil movements for the slow-pitch stride produce a much more exaggerated motion (some great hitters such as Kirby Puckett of the Minnesota Twins also have this style, with no ill effects because it obviously is comfortable for them), but most hitters should very "quietly" move their front foot so they will keep everything in balance.

Good Stride Can Mean Good Hip Action

The stride action toward the pitcher really begins a series of body actions that will eventually open up the hips. And I firmly believe that the action of the hips is a key to good hitting, something that the great Hall of Fame slugger Ted Williams always preached. He sold me on

FIGURE 7-2A

FIGURE 7-2B

FIGURE 7-2E

FIGURE 7-2F

FIGURE 7-2C

FIGURE 7-2D

FIGURE 7-2G

PUCKETT POWER STRIDE:
Named for Minnesota Twins'
slugger Kirby Puckett (because of
its similarity), this stride helps
prevent overstriding and aids in
generating power. The batter
picks up his front foot and sets it
down in nearly the exact position.
This helps generate a pronounced
hip turn and weight shift by
keeping firm pressure between
the ball of the rear foot and the
ground (Feel Point #10). Because
this stride produces a more severe
squat, thus lowering the rear
shoulder markedly, it can more
often be successfully used in slow
pitch to produce those long fly
balls that fly over the fence.

it, too, because I've looked at the sequence from every possible angle and the good hip action is an indelible part of good hitting.

But don't be so conscious of what the hips are doing that you forget all the other actions. In a nutshell, if you stride properly and maintain the slight angle in the front knee, the swinging action of the arms and the pivoting of the rear foot will accelerate the hips for a powerful swing.

Practicing the drills with the feel points will play a large part in putting everything together, but unless the stride is perfect, it really won't matter too much what the hips are doing. Stride first for a firm foundation, and the arms and hips will follow right through the contact with the ball and into the follow-through position. If you worry about the hips and forget the stride, nothing will happen. So concentrate on keeping the stride consistent and as short as is comfortable for you.

With experience and a mastery of the stride will come the ability to focus more on the hip action. For example, if you are a pull hitter and have trouble making contact, you can open the stance a bit, maintain the top half inward "coil," get closer to the plate and be very quick with the bat to regain your form. But worry about those little tricks only after you've perfected your stride.

Plant That Stride Foot

The stride really is not complete until that front foot is firmly planted with a slightly angled locked front knee. This provides a balance point to receive the power transferred from the rear foot during the accelerated swinging actions of both arms. Too often hitters overstride by not planting the foot correctly or straightening out the front leg prior to contact. As a result, they have a poor foundation for the lower half of the body and simply will not hit the ball very well, if at all. The first three feel points will help you get a grasp of hitting posture.

There are two other check points to help you learn the proper stride. Grip the surface with the toes as if picking up a marble or squeezing a towel. This will give you a sense of the entire front leg being strong and braced. Secondly, raise the front knee twelve inches or more and balance on the rear bent knee. Then plant the stride foot and grip the ground surface with the toes.

All of this is part of the transfer of power from the rear to the front foot. To make if effective, you must have the rear foot firmly planted in the batter's box before striding. This allows the weight to rest on that foot (with the pressure felt in the big toe area) before the stride and swing begins. Bend the knees slightly because this will help to

FIGURE 7-3A

FIGURE 7-3B

FIGURE 7-3C

TAKING A PITCH: *The key to taking a pitch is keeping the eyes on the ball throughout and the front foot closed (7-3C), thus keeping the hips closed and hands and weight back, always ready to launch the bat if the pitch is to be swung at. 7-3A through 7-3C show a movement that is identical to one that will result in a swing. In 7-3D, the batter has decided not to swing, yet continues to keep his eyes on the oncoming pitch. (7-3E through 7-3G).*

FIGURE 7-3D

FIGURE 7-3F

FIGURE 7-3E

FIGURE 7-3G

generate the power to shift the weight from the rear foot to the front foot by pushing against the surface while pivoting from the inside of the ball of the foot. That also gives you some flexibility to move away from inside pitches or to try and pull the ball. If your knees are too stiff, there will be little flexibility to make those adjustments.

Keep the weight back on that rear foot until you decide to swing at the ball. Once you make the commitment, move the weight from the rear to the front hip by pivoting as quickly as possible. Swinging at the precise time will automatically trigger the power switch and open the hips.

The key rule when transferring the weight from the back to the front foot is that the bat should meet the ball when the weight is transferred to the front foot. Do it and you will hit the ball hard; if you don't, you won't.

Transferring the Weight

The road to a good weight transfer begins by keeping the top half of the body leaning in a bit of a downward motion as that front leg moves and grips the surface. That downward motion with the front knee locked in a slightly angled position will keep the hip from opening too soon, possibly raising it, along with the front shoulder and head. If the front knee straightens out prior to contact with the ball, the weight is apt to stay on the rear foot, preventing a weight transfer.

If you fail to initiate a straight line action by the knee coupled with a slight roll of the hips, then your body will fly upward and out of the hitting zone. Your eyes also will be pulled up and you will lose the sharp focus you must keep on the ball as it zooms toward the plate. Lose sight of the ball and you simply won't have time to refocus on it. A potential hitting opportunity is then lost.

The hitter must concentrate on a short stride and heel plant while the body weight remains stationary. Here are some drills that also will help you do this.

1. Stride with the front foot. Plant it, then pivot on the rear foot to transfer the weight to the front. Feel the stretch in the top portion of the front leg, slightly below the front hip. (See Dead Foot Stride Pivot Drill.)

2. Hold the bat with the front arm straight out, and throw a ball beneath it in a straight path, and feel the pivot and transfer of weight. (See Sidearm Throw.)

3. Hold the bat against the front of the thighs. Stride and plant the front foot, then feel the rear hip movement. The rear hip will move the

FIGURE 7-4A   **FIGURE 7-4B**

STRIDE/PIVOT DRILL: *Assume stance with bat tucked behind back and parallel to ground. Take normal stride and pull with rear arm, turning the rear hip as quickly as possible. The pivot, or rotation of hips, should move the shoulders at least 90 degrees and as much as 180 degrees (shoulder replacing shoulder) from starting position.*

front hip after its slight movement following the stride. Do not allow the front knee to snap back; the rear hip will begin to propel the bat.

Faults

1. *Not keeping the ball of the rear foot on the ground.* This creates an improper foundation and inhibits the proper upper body acceleration because resistance is not set in the feet for the swinging actions of the upper half of the body.

2. *Body moves forward.* This causes improper weight transfer, a tendency to lunge, and visual problems tracking the ball to the hitting zone.

3. *Weight on the front foot.* This prevents the hitter's adjustment to off-speed pitches. The rear foot does not pivot thus there is no transfer of weight with a subsequent lack of power.

FIGURE 7-5

STRIDE/PIVOT AND SHOULDER-EXCHANGE DRILL: *This is similar to the "Stride/Pivot Drill" except that the bat is held behind the shoulders. The goal of this drill is to completely exchange the positions of the shoulders, that is, the rear shoulder should rotate until it reaches the starting position of the front shoulder, which in turn should rotate 180 degrees into the starting position of the rear shoulder.*

4. *Incorrect angling of the front foot.* If the toes are straight ahead instead of at a forty-five-degree angle, the plant foot will open the front hip too soon, making it difficult to hit the outside pitch. A square foot-toe alignment also has a tendency to lock the hip, preventing it from opening naturally during the transfer process.

5. *Front knee is not bent properly.* This causes a locking of he front knee and lifts your vision off the ball as it heads toward the plate.

6. *Lead leg straightens prior to contact.* This also changes the visual tracking of the ball and the weight will probably stay on the rear foot, preventing the proper transfer.

7. *Front knee bent downward.* This also lowers the eyes from tracking the ball.

FIGURE 7-6A

FIGURE 7-6B

STRIDE: *The first variation of the stride is the curl (7-6B), which is a mini-coiling by the front leg, hips, and upper body. The second variation is raised step (also known as the Puckett Power Stride), as demonstrated in 7-6C. The most common stride is the glide step (7-6D), which moves the front foot forward quietly and low to the ground. The mid-stripe shown in the photos is used to determine the correct position of the rear knee upon execution of the stride, swing and follow-through: It should not go forward of this line.*

FIGURE 7-6C

FIGURE 7-6D

FIGURE 7-7A

FIGURE 7-7C

FIGURE 7-7B

SIDEARM THROW: From a normal stance, lift and hold with the front arm the bat away from the body, covering the hitting area; then toss the ball side-arm while keeping the bat as close as possible to the starting positon. This drill simulates the proper lowering and driving of the rear shoulder through the hitting area. It also helps the player feel "hitting against a firm, rigid frontside," one of the batting tenets first advanced by the late hitting guru Charley Lau.

VIII. The Swing

There are three very important ingredients neded to hit a soft-ball—the upper half of your body, the lower half of your body and your bat. The bat you can buy, but as far as your body goes, you're stuck with what you were born with, and you must learn how to develop the proper techniques for using it. In fast-pitch softball, as in baseball, there are two distinct types of hitters—the hitter who utilizes running speed to get on base and the power swing hitter, who always hits the ball hard.

Some fast-pitch softball hitters are "top half hitters," though many times this might look like a lunge at the ball, with the weight on the front foot before contact. What the good hitters do is to stride and transfer the weight to the front foot with very little rear foot and hip action, and they add great timing and solid contact downward. This type of contact invariably produces ground balls.

To hit a fast-pitch softball, the bat must travel in an arc and finish on a straight path to the ball, particularly for pitches between the lower part of the rib cage and middle of the thighs. The distance of that arc and how far the bat must travel is determined by where the hands start swinging, and this varies with each hitter.

We hear much about "swinging down" at a pitch. This really means the hitter takes the bat down slightly to eliminate the weight of the bat, and then the bat moves forward with the hands positioned in the palm down/palm up position.

The top hand actually pushes the bottom hand slightly downward. This is feel point 8. As the hands move forward, the bottom hand is palm down and the top hand, which has the knuckles in split alignment, turns so that the palms are facing upward. This is when the arc for the bat barrel is created behind the rear shoulder. The hands on the bat are moving rapidly by the action of both elbows accelerating both forearms into full arm extension upon contact with the ball. The grip pressure increases by squeezing the last three fingers of each hand to create a muscular contraction in the forearms, as in feel point 9.

Waiting to Swing

Before you are able to swing a bat, you have to deal with the pitcher. The minutes and seconds before the ball comes seem interminable, but the following are a few tips to make it easier:

57

FIGURE 8-1A

FIGURE 8-1E

FIGURE 8-1B

FIGURE 8-1F

FIGURE 8-1C

FIGURE 8-1D

FIGURE 8-1G

POWER SWING—DEAD FOOT STRIDE: *The batter makes a slow, short and soft planting of the front foot (8-1A through 8-1C). Pressure is felt along the inner edge of the planted foot, and the 45° angle of the front leg to the upper body is maintained. The pull/push movement from the coil position begins in 8-1E. The hands make the shortest possible arc, propelling the barrel of the bat into the path of the ball.*

FIGURE 8-1H

POWER SWING—PRONATE AND SUPINATE: *8-1H through 8-1J show the bottom hand pronating, or turning the palm downward, and the top*

FIGURE 8-1J

FIGURE 8-1I

hand supinating, or turning the palm upward and away from the body.
At the same time, the pressure on the ball of the rear foot allows the

FIGURE 8-1K

FIGURE 8-1L

hips to open quickly, thus increasing bat speed and ultimately resulting in more power. As in a good golf swing, the elbow of the top hand

FIGURE 8-1N

FIGURE 8-1M

drives down and close to the rear hip, and then, ideally, into full extension as contact is made.

1. When the pitcher retrieves the ball, focus on some part of his or her body, but don't look into the eyes.

2. While you are waiting for the delivery of the ball, look at the pitcher's chest or concentrate and listen to yourself breathe, without any deep thought processes. Too many hitters outthink themselves during those few seconds between pitches.

3. As pitcher sets for delivery, shift your eyes to the pitcher's hips. See the arm coming and pick up the ball's flight. This eliminates picking up a pitcher's body movements and focuses your eyes on the ball as much as possible.

Get Some Elbow Room

Part of being a good hitter is learning how to use every inch of your arms, from shoulder to wrist, every time you swing the bat. That primarily means getting the fullest acceleration of the bat barrel to the extension with the arms so that you can put the greatest force possible into your swing and contact with the ball.

There are several elements involved in that extension process. Start with feel point 5 by placing the thumb of the top hand against

FIGURE 8-1O

FIGURE 8-1P

FIGURE 8-1Q

POWER SWING—FOLLOW THROUGH: 8-1O through 8-1Q show the completion of the swing. The batter should feel a stretch extension of the muscles at the top of the thigh in the front leg and a stretch along the muscles of rear shoulder and back of the arm of the top hand.

the top outer edge of the shoulders, and raise the bat up two or three inches and away four to six inches. Both shoulders and arms are turned inwards to form a coil position. You must concentrate on the proper positioning of your elbows. The front elbow can be droppd slightly or kept in a parallel position with the ground while the rear elbow is slightly higher. This position will eventually produce a quicker swing and you will be better able to meet the ball in front of you.

Of course, there are some hitters who say they are more comfortable with their elbows higher or lower than the levels I have just outlined, but there is little doubt that the most productive hitters always have their front elbow positioned in the middle of their body. Raising the elbows too high creates the need to move the elbows downward as you prepare to swing the bat, particularly going after lower pitches. That, in turn, creates a longer, slower swing. If the elbows are too low, you obviously must bring them up to the rear shoulder area to make a correct swing. In both cases, this involves one more movement that you must make within the split second you have to swing the bat. That split second can make a difference in the decision-making process or in the mechanics of the swing.

One last admonition that applies to all body movements: if you are comfortable, consistent and productive with positions other than I have outlined, then by all means stay with them. Why spoil a good thing? But if you are comfortable but not consistent nor productive, then you should change and endure any discomfort that is part of finding a new posture.

Get Those Arms Fully Extended

Extension is using the arms to move the bat into position to make contact with the ball. All discussions on fully extending the arms when hitting can begin and end with one principle: When the arms are fully extended on the swing, you have a better chance of hitting the ball hard. That's really all you need to look for—to hit the ball hard and have a good opportunity for a base hit. This applies to pull hitters and those wishing to hit to the opposite field.

Once the arms are fully extended, the elbows, hands and wrists will be locked tightly to the forearms.

Get the Shoulders Involved

Without the shoulders providing a rotary movement, it would be difficult to extend the arms and get any power behind the swing.

FIGURE 8-2A

FIGURE 8-2B

FIGURE 8-2E

FIGURE 8-2F

FIGURE 8-2C

FIGURE 8-2D

FIGURE 8-2G

POWER SWING AT HIGH STRIKE:
The ideal swing plane keeps the barrel of the bat in the plane of the oncoming ball throughout the critical zone of contact. This can vary from six to eight inches, depending on the type of pitch.

FIGURE 8-3A

FIGURE 8-3E

FIGURE 8-3B

FIGURE 8-3E

FIGURE 8-3C

FIGURE 8-3D

FIGURE 8-3G

**POWER SWING, SLOW PITCH—
HITTING THE HIGH STRIKE:** *This
sequence clearly shows the action
of the rear shoulder, which drives
down, through the hitting area
(with the elbow tucked close to
the rear hip as shown in 8-3E). As
shown in 8-3F, the power or long
ball swing must meet the
oncoming pitch just below or at
shoulder level for maximum drive
and lift.*

FIGURE 8-4A

HIGH STRIKE HANDS POSITON: *The batter keeps the hands and swing plane of the barrel of the bat in the path of the oncoming ball by making*

FIGURE 8-4C

FIGURE 8-4B

a direct path from the ready or launch position to the contact point.

Faulty shoulder positioning causes more problems than most hitters realize. The worst thing you can do is to dip your rear shoulder too much and then drop your hands. The rear elbow drops with them, the front elbow and shoulder flies upward and out too soon, and you just uppercut the ball. You'll miss or just hit a high fly ball.

The shoulders must work consistently in sequence with the hips, arms and hands. The shoulders and arms should remain relaxed as the grip pressure on the bat handle increases and the arms move to the proper extension. That relaxation is necessary so the upper half of your body won't tense up and provide resistance to the shoulders/arms/hands/bat/hip rotation.

You may find it favorable to begin the inward rotation of the rear shoulder (while still maintaining the ninety-degree front arm angle) prior to the pitcher's releasing the ball. This will move the hands and arms into a ready position and eliminate a critical timing factor associated with the stride and inward rotation. I point this out because some hitters have difficulty striding and rotating inwardly at the same time while keeping their timing to hit the oncoming ball.

Once you have rotated your shoulders inwardly—or coiled them— you must swing the bat in a direct diagonal line and on a plane that brings it into full contact with the ball. The rear elbow will be the

FIGURE 8-5

FULL EXTENSION: *The ideal swing produces contact at full extension of the arms. The batter will* **always** *hit a line drive when contacting the middle of the ball at full extension.*

guiding force in this movement, moving two or three inches toward the body, as the front arm starts pulling the bat along the plane to the ball.

Remember, although the shoulders do not remain even throughout the swing, you should make a conscious effort to keep them level, or even moving slightly downward, until you plant the front foot. Then drive that front shoulder slightly up and out and the rear shoulder down and through the hitting zone until it replaces the position of the front shoulder.

You cannot ignore the pivot of the rear foot, either. As the arms, shoulders and hands come into action after the stride, the rear foot pivot starts and turns the rear vertical half of the body. This aids the acceleration of the arms, shoulders, hands and bat, and continues to follow the swing. You either turn completely to square the hips for an inside pitch or move a quarter turn to position the rear shoulder and hip to face and hit to the opposite field.

Once the ball is hit, the top hand rolls over the bottom hand into a follow-through. The bat either goes to a forty-five-degree angle upwards or ends up slightly below the shoulder after both arms have folded at the elbow.

At Last, the Swing

Swinging a bat is a very individual thing, and we've all seen that as we watched baseball players through the year. In the major leagues, for example, there is the big, picture-perfect swing of Mark McGwire of the Oakland A's, something that is worth watching whether or not he hits the ball. There is also Gary Gaetti of the Minnesota Twins who has a reputation of waiting as long as any hitter in baseball on a pitch, but he can do that because he has a very compact swing that is like a blur when he launches it.

The same applies to fast-pitch softball. Like major league hitters, fast-pitch softball hitters should strive to develop a line drive type of swing before they ever worry about hitting home runs. If you develop a swing that produces hard hit balls, the big dingers will come. So will the other hits that zoom into the outfield on a line or skip through the infield so fast that fielders are unable to get them.

There is one constant about the art of swinging a bat: except for pitches that are exactly waist high for a dead level swing, nineteen out of twenty pitches never will be where the hitter expects, and he or she will have to move the bat up or down to hit them. But despite this, you can develop a smooth level swing that will get the bat on the ball and produce solid contact. You must concentrate on keeping the head level as the ball is tracked, and be sure to keep the bat level throughout the swing, regardless of where the ball is located. A smooth swing is never bothered by the ball's location.

In fast-pitch softball, for instance, the down-swing is used as a variation technique to get a good piece of the ball. Some pitchers throw with great velocity and their "*rise ball*" is very effective. You can cope with this by positioning your hands slightly below the barrel of the bat and adjusting your swing so the barrel would be slightly above the hands on contact with the ball. You must remember to swing down so you can produce either a line drive or a hard grounder.

If the ball is low, you must maintain a direct diagonal swing, with the hands slightly higher as the bat comes downward and the palm down/palm up position occurs, putting the top hand below the bottom hand. Both then move laterally and take the bat barrel upwards and through the ball.

If the ball is inside, you must open the hips quickly to a squared position, and the hands are behind the barrel at full arm extension when it makes contact with the ball. The hips should be squared to the pitcher, and the rear shoulder replaces the lead shoulder in supplying power.

If the ball is outside, the hands are ahead of the bat but the hips are not open as far as for the inside pitch, perhaps about forty-five degrees. Contact with the ball occurs after it has passed the front edge of the plate, and the rear shoulder will finish in a direct line with

FIGGURE 8-6A   **FIGURE 8-6B**

CHOP SWING: *This swing requires the arms and shoulders to do the majority of the work in making contact. The batter makes a near-total*

FIGURE 8-6E

FIGURE 8-6C

FIGURE 8-6D

transfer of weight to the front foot before making contact. The lower half of the body is successfully disengaged by diminishing the pressure

FIGURE 8-6F

FIGURE 8-6G

applied by the ball of the rear foot. The object of this swing is to hit the ball on the ground and utilize the batter's foot speed to get on base.

FIGURE 8-6I

FIGURE 8-6H

FIGURE 8-6J

FIGURE 8-6K

FIGURE 8-6M

FIGURE 8-6L

FIGURE 8-6N

FIGURE 8-7A

POWER SWING AT LOW STRIKE: *The batter shows excellent lateral (8-7B & 8-7C) and rotary movement (Photos 8-7D through 8-7G) while*

FIGURE 8-7C

FIGURE 8-7B

lowering the body via a slight squat, to get the rear shoulder into position for its powerful drive down and through the contact zone. The

FIGURE 8-7D

FIGURE 8-7E

ball of the rear foot maintains constant pressure throughout the swing, thus enabling the hips to open quickly.

FIGURE 8-7G

FIGURE 8-7F

FIGURE 8-8

LOW PITCH BAT POSITION: *The batter maintains good rear shoulder position, driving down and through the hitting area. The hands are above the level of the pitch when contact is made.*

INSIDE PITCH BAT POSITION: *In hitting an inside pitch, the hips must open as quickly as possible to allow the shoulder, arms and hands to literally whip the barrel of the bat ahead of the hands to meet the ball. Without this rapid hip rotation, the bat will arrive in the contact area a split-second too late and the batter will be jammed.*

FIGURE 8-9

FIGURE 8-10

OUTSIDE PITCH BAT POSITION: *When hitting an outside pitch, the batter contacts the ball with the hands leading the barrel of the bat through the hitting area. The front shoulder does not have as far to rotate before striking the outside pitch.*

HIGH PITCH BAT POSITON: The ideal best position for contact is with the barrel slightly higher than the hands; this gets the bat in the path of the concoming ball quicker and keeps it there longer. It also prevents raising the front elbow too high, which lowers the barrel as it moves through the hitting zone. Result: a popped ball or complete miss.

FIGURE 8-11

FIGURE 8-12

WAIST-HIGH PITCH BAT POSITION: For most batters, this is the "wheel-house" spot—where one can turn most efficiently and quickly and generate the most bat speed. Power hitters should practice driving this pitch into the air (and over the fence) while spray hitters should hit this pitch hard on the ground into the infield holes.

FIGURE 8-13A

POSITION OF BARREL/LOW PITCH: *In making contact with a low pitch (8-13B) the batter makes a slight squat—lowering the arms and hands—to help keep the arc of the swing in the plane of the oncoming ball as*

FIGURE 8-13C

FIGURE 8-13B

long as possible. However, for pitches below the waist, the barrel of the bat is always lower than the hands.

the direction of the ball to the opposite field, instead of exchanging positions with the front shoulder as it does on an inside pitch. The toes of the rear foot and the rear hip should be pointing to opposite fields once the ball has been hit.

If the ball comes in letter-high, you merely place the hands a little lower than the bat barrel, trying to swing on a slight downward plane after the pitch. Try not to swing at the rise ball. Hitters often raise the front elbow, causing the bat to drop. If this happens, though the swing is level, it will be very weak.

Despite all these instructions, don't always be changing your swing, particularly when you change your position in the batter's box. It is okay to adjust the hands up or down, but any significant changes with your stride and body position as it relates to the inside edge of the plate should be made with extreme care. This enables you to hit to all fields. If you want to hit to the *opposite field*, move away from the plate slightly, close your stance and stride slightly toward the inside edge of the plate to hit the outside pitch to the opposite field. You still have enough room to pull an inside pitch. You give away the plate to the pitcher but get it right back by striding into the pitch. If you wish to *pull the ball*, put your back foot closer to the plate and assume an open or square stance, whichever feels more comfortable. Don't shift your hands or change your swing because the foot position change will take care of everything. And by all means be quick with the bat! If you need to *hit the ball on the ground* in a hit-and-run, swing the bat on a slightly downward plane.

And finally a word about something to which I just referred—*the quick bat*. This is produced by quick hands and quick hips. Since the hands trail in the swing sequence, keep them back until the weight goes over to the front foot and the hips begin to open. Then let them fly. But don't transfer your weight to the front foot and then try to decide whether to swing. Once that weight hits the front foot, you are committed and you must slam into the ball.

With pitches coming from a relatively close distance in fast-pitch softball, you must be quick, but you also must be realistic. If you face a power pitcher, there is little chance of getting a ball to pull, so you must be prepared to handle the pitch that is delivered. Make the mental reservation to be quick with the bat, wait as long as possible for the pitch, keep your hands back and then go after the ball. Part of being realistic also acknowledges that a particular pitcher may give you problems. Acknowledge them and find another way to succeed, such as going to the opposite field.

Hitting Faults

1. *Slow, sweeping swing.* This is caused by the following:
   (a) Bat barrel too low;
   (b) Poor inward rotation of the shoulders;
   (c) Front elbow not bent at a ninety-degree angle at the beginning of swing;
   (d) Hands not moving in direct diagonal line to ball; or
   (e) Lead shoulder open too soon.
2. *Loss of power.* This is caused by the following:
   (a) Poor inward rotation of the shoulders;
   (b) Failure to pivot on rear foot, forcing your arms to supply everything;
   (c) Lead shoulder opens too soon and will produce a weakness to hit an outside pitch; or
   (d) Palm of the top hand not facing upward.
3. *Hitching.* The hands move up or down as the pitch nears the strike zone, and that movement hinders getting the arms into full extension, thus curtailing both bat speed and timing.
4. *Barrel drag.* The elbow of the rear arm is too high, causing the barrel to drop slightly and increasing the distance to contact the ball.
5. *Hitting balls into the ground.* Both arms and hands are swinging the bat downward and contacting the top part of the ball, causing the power to go downward.
6. *Rear leg collapses.* The power is taken away from the rear hip acceleration process for the arms.

7. *Weight resting on rear foot.* This causes a lowering of the rear knee, creating a looping swing and a collapse of the knee.

8. *Rear elbow too high at beginning of swing.* The elbow drops down, causing the bat to drop and increasing the distance to the ball's contact point.

9. *Head and eyes are not level.* You cannot focus both eyes on the ball to hit it.

10. *Front elbow moves up.* The bat will drop from its swing arc.

11. *Lead elbow bends before arc is finished.* The head has moved the bat toward the body, not through the ball.

12. *Wrists roll before contact.* The arc principle has been violated.

The Follow-Through

As Yogi Berra once said about everything, "It's not over till it's over." And in this case, we are talking about the swing, because the swing isn't over until you complete your follow-through motion. Once the bat has struck the ball, it cannot stop. You must complete the full arc of the swing before dropping the bat and beginning to run. Nor, as we noted earlier in the book, should you release either of your hands from the bat until that arc is completed. You need them to generate as much power and direction as possible. Too often balls that are solidly struck simply lose their force because a hitter stops the swing once the bat makes contact.

IX. Bunting and Hitting to All Fields

Bunting a ball and playing softball are not always linked because the popular conception of softball is a sport of big, booming hits. Yet the fast-pitch softball game approximates hardball in many aspects, and it really is a tighter game when there is great pitching. So, bunting must be considered a very integral part of the game's strategical aspects, and its merits never can be discounted.

Thus, the "short game" in fast-pitch softball encompasses the traditional square-around bunt, bunting from the hitting position, and drag bunting for a base hit. It also includes slap hitting, where a batter slides his top hand, or both hands, one-third of the way up the handle of the bat and tries to knock the ball past the two corners— the first and third basemen—who may be playing in to take away the bunt.

Bunting in order to move a base runner into scoring position does not have to mean a sacrifice for the bunter. Performed properly, it also can easily become a base hit. Hitters who make up their mind to bunt can follow the ball better because they won't have to worry about swinging; they can just focus on the ball itself and place it properly on their bat. The infielders' placement—in at the corners to take away the bunt—also offers the hitter more territory toward the shortstop and second base areas in which to place the ball.

The Body's Role

You must keep the following points in mind when you decide to bunt:

1. *Stance.* The body should be forward in the front of the batter's box, giving you an opportunity to get the ball into fair territory. When the pitcher separates his hands prior to releasing the ball, place the front foot away from the inside of the batter's box, and bring the rear foot up to a parallel position in the box. Keep the body low, with the knees bent, and as still as possible to create a small strike zone.

2. *Plate coverage.* As the body is squaring, place the bottom hand up the bat an inch or two and the top hand a third of the way up the bat barrel to a position slightly below the trademark. The ring and little fingers of this hand form a platform upon which sits the index

finger. The bat rests on that, supported by the thumb, which is turned sideways. The bottom hand also exerts more pressure on the bat, which is held away from the body. The top hand holds the bat in a V-shape near the trademark, but not too tightly. The top hand should never be lower than the bottom hand. A good example where this could happen is on a low, outside pitch where the handle is higher than the barrel. Keep the bat at a forty-five-degree angle.

3. *Direction.* If you want to bunt toward first base, push the bottom hand forward, angling the barrel of the bat backward. If you wish to bunt toward third base—and this is preferable with a runner on first base—bring the bottom hand toward the body to form the proper angle. Remember, if the first and third basemen really are hard chargers, it is possible to push the ball past them by straightening the arms, tightening the grip and pushing the barrel toward the ball, without any recoil upon contact with the ball. A potential sacrifice can then become a base hit.

Types of Bunts

In fast-pitch softball, I advocate bunting from the hitting position instead of the square-around method because there simply isn't time to square away and take aim at the ball. The release of the ball by the pitcher in fast-pitch is much more abbreviated than in baseball where the batter can square around once the pitcher's front foot is picked up.

However, if you choose to use the *square-around method*, then your knees must be low once that position is established. Be certain, too, that the arms are in a semi-angled and locked position at the elbows. The bat is held without firm pressure because a loose grip, with the elbows back, absorbs the ball's collision with the bat and causes the ball to die or slow down quicker once it hits the ground. Ideally, contact is made with the lower half of the bat contacting the upper half of the ball to force the ball straight down before it begins rolling. If the bat is held too firmly, then the ball will ricochet quicker to a fielder.

In bunting from the *hitting position*, put the bat around and into the path of the ball, and allow the rear knee to go inwards toward the front knee as the top half of the body turns toward the pitcher. The ball is contacted in front of the plate, and the top half of the bat should make contact with the bottom half of the ball, with both elbows bending together and drawing the bat slightly backward to cushion the ball's contact.

Another type is a *drag bunt*. Hold the bat the same way you do for a sacrifice, again being careful not to have it in a tight grip after sliding the top hand up the bat to a proper angle for ball placement.

But instead of drawing back the bat when striking the ball, push it forward a bit. A left-handed hitter will actually stride with the front foot, delaying the start a bit to try and hold the infielders at their positions, and then cross the rear foot over the front foot. At this point, the body is momentarily stationary before the hitter angles the barrel for ball placement and takes off. Try to avoid the rear leg over the front as a continuous movement.

Right-handed hitters must wait a split second longer before committing to the bunt, until the ball is almost to the plate. You must be certain to get the bat in front of the plate, held loosely as in the sacrifice mode. Keep the front foot in place and bent, and drop the rear foot toward the outside line of the batter's box.

To execute a *push bunt*, you must set up in the rear of the batter's box. As the pitcher releases the ball, open the front foot, then cross over, and plant the rear foot. Slide the top hand up the bat near the trademark, and while it is by the side of the head, slap the ball to the shortstop area or second base. Contact with the ball must be made as either foot is inside the front line of the batter's box, though the actual motion is almost a controlled run out of the box.

The *slap hit* or *fake bunt and hit* is a fine technique for softball players of both sexes, particularly when they must cope with a speed pitcher who can dominate an entire lineup. The objective is to make contact with the ball and hit it anyplace there is a big hole as infielders move to cover the bases on hit-and-runs and sacrifice situations. With active first and third basemen, a hitter with good bat control has a marvelous opportunity to drive the ball past them (the ultimate results may be a bit more temerity in charging bunts, also opening up more of those opportunities).

As soon as the pitcher presents the ball, show a bunt without squaring up, and read quickly whether the first and third basemen are beginning to charge the plate. If they are, quickly bring the bat back to the outer edge of the shoulder. Move the bottom hand up the bat about three inches and slide the top hand down to meet it.

When bringing the bat to the shoulder, leave the front shoulder open for a better chance to slash the ball and get it to the shortstop area of the infield. The act of slashing should be a short, controlled swing. A right-handed hitter does not have to show bunt, but can just slide the top hand up the bat and bring it forward with the top hand, thus pushing the bat forward for contact. A left-handed hitter, being closer to first base, can cheat a bit by dragging or pushing the bunt.

You can freeze the fielders by striding, as if you were going to hit, before slapping at the ball, simply by coming forward a bit with the front foot after a half pivot with the rear foot. Also bring the hand up the bat to get the proper angle to slap the ball toward first or third base. Remember, all you want to do is make contact with the ball on your first step, so don't leave the batter's box early, as you might in a drag bunt situation, and don't cross the legs over.

If you are a right-handed hitter and wish to slash the ball past the shortstop, leave the shoulder open; if you want it going past second base, close the shoulder and drag the barrel.

Factors to Consider

There are also some considerations in using these techniques, and they deal mainly with the situation created by the defense and the mental agility of the hitter.

1. Defensive alignment by the corners. If they are positioned in, or back, and there are runners on base, then they should be considered along with the hitter's abilities, including speed, as well as the game situation (outs, inning, score, hitters upcoming, pitcher).

2. The hitter's ability to read the defense.

3. How fast the pitcher is throwing.

4. The ability of the hitter to place the ball toward the shortstop and second base area.

In considering these variables, the hitter may read and show bunt but, once the pitcher either presents the ball or separates it from his glove, go to the slap technique.

Hitting to the Opposite Field

Throughout the book, I have made frequent references to using batting techniques to hit to the opposite field. It is done quite frequently in baseball and gives a hitter another weapon.

Hitting to the opposite field is more difficult in fast-pitch softball than in baseball, pretty much an individual skill that still should be worked on in practice if only to give every hitter another weapon to cope with certain kinds of pitches. For one thing, it takes away a defense's advantage of specific positioning of its fielders; for another, it increases a player's hitting area and provides a wider array of balls that can be attacked; and for a third, it reduces strikeouts by giving a hitter a chance to attack pitches from the middle third to the outer third of the plate. Hitters also won't have to worry about pulling every pitch or waiting for one they can pull. This will also help to develop the ability to hit the outside pitch with less of a turn than is necessary to pull the inside pitch.

As an example of what this can do for team offense, consider a couple of possible situations:

1. With a man on first base, a right-handed hitter strokes a hit into right field, and the baserunner makes it to third base, drawing a throw from the right-fielder, and enabling the hitter to make second base. Now runners are on second and third and in scoring position.

2. A runner is on first and a right-handed hitter strokes a hit into right field, sending the runner to third base. The runners are on first and third, with the latter in scoring position on any number of possible situations.

3. With a runner on first and a right-handed hitter up, the second baseman shades toward bag. The hitter goes to the opposite field, forcing the fielder to make an off-balance stop. This quells a possible double play.

When and How to Make It Happen

You must be aware of the count. You can take the first pitch the opposite way, or you can do it on 1-0, 1-1, 2-0, 2-1, 3-1. The ball with most two-strike counts, however, looks like a pea, and psychological disadvantages come into play. In all instances, though, you should shorten up your swing and certainly refrain from trying to pull the ball. As we noted in discussing the swing, move away from the plate, close the stance slightly and get more of an angle on where you wish to hit. All the pitches will be away from you but you still can get good, solid contact and drive the ball with a compact swing.

If you are facing a flame-throwing pitcher, forget about pulling the ball and be content to go with the best pitch, regardless of what it may be, and wait as long as possible with your hands back before launching a quick bat. That is good advice when facing any pitcher who presents a constant problem. Give him the plate at the outset. Then you need not worry about pulling the ball, because all the pitches will be away from you and easier to hit. You can shorten up your swing and reclaim that plate by striding into the ball.

X. Slow-Pitch Hitting

A More Relaxed Game

The fun version of the game of softball is slow-pitch. It is the one American sport for the ages, and most of all, it is fun to play because it is not difficult to hit the ball. How far a hitter can run is something else and so is catching it, but isn't that part of the fun of the game?

Consider some of the merits of playing the game:

1. There are slow-pitch professional leagues which reward good players with contracts and salaries.

2. There are thousands of recreational amateur leagues, at various levels of competition, that provide great outlets for the men and women who once played baseball or fast-pitch softball but find their instincts, reactions and skills diminished by age even though their love of hitting a ball is stronger than ever.

3. Then there are the simple recreational players. These include the players who grab a bat and ball and round up friends to play a bit, or the families who get together at picnics and have some fun with the game.

While the idea is to have fun, there also is nothing wrong with adding to one's enjoyment by increasing the skill level. For example, some players get down because while they hit the ball, it just goes straight up in the air to the fielders or down on the ground toward infielders. Remember, softball has ten fielders, so getting a ball into the open spaces is no dead-eye cinch.

The ultimate means of success is timing the hitting actions with the pitch, regardless of whether it is high or low. You not only must have the correct timing to hit the ball, but you must also know how to get the best part of the bat on the ball and then project as much power as possible to the precise part of the ball.

We start with one simple premise. Everyone can hit against a slowly pitched softball. In this section, we want to show you how to do it better and with a consistent technique that will make a fun game even more so. Much of the technique that applied to the fast-pitch hitting also applies with slow-pitch. The biggest differences will be found in the stride, the coil of the shoulders and the swing, and how they must be adjusted to hit that big melon of a ball that gets lobbed up to the plate.

Getting Ready

You can do nothing correctly until you are prepared to hit, and this means being comfortably set in the batter's box with the feet, knees, upper body and the position of the bat, including the grip, all in proper order. We call this getting the body in the hitting posture with "plate coverage." While the rules are a bit strict for baseball and fast-pitch softball, they are not as big a factor in slow-pitch because you will have time to step and position the body in relationship to how the ball is approaching the plate.

In slow-pitch, you will have time to (1) move the front foot away from the edge of the plate to pull the inside ball, (2) step toward the plate to hit to the opposite field, or (3) stride straight and just position the arms and bat on the ball in the strike zone. You also will have enough time to pick up whatever spins the pitcher has put on the ball and have enough time to adjust to it.

Gripping the Bat

We discussed the specific elements of gripping the bat in Chapter V and the use of the hands in Chapter VI, but when looking at slow-pitch hitting, you really have two choices—the end grip or the modified choke grip. In slow-pitch softball, power hitters want to hold the bat at the end of the handle so they can get as much of it into the ball as possible. Line drive hitters may choke up because the bat may be too heavy, or they feel in better control. But if the situation calls for a hit to win a game, everyone should choke up, because it gives you a better chance of controlling the barrel weight and contacting the ball near the waist to produce a line drive instead of a pop up or fly ball. Of course, end-of-the-bat hitters may not feel comfortable choking up and may be better able to crank out a hit in their regular position.

Striding Into a Slow Pitch

Hitting in slow-pitch softball requires many of the same principles that we covered in the fast-pitch game. Again, the "feel points" come in to play as a good means to check on whether the proper motions are being used. The speed on the ball, however, allows for several meaningful variations simply because the hitter has more time to see the ball and move his body to adjust to it.

In slow pitch, you may move the feet around into different positions before swinging without any grave consequences. Where can they go?

1. From the stationary position, with good plate coverage and the front foot dividing the middle of the plate, move the front foot (as a right-handed hitter) toward third base if you want to pull the ball into left field. A left-handed hitter would stride toward first base.

2. Stride straight ahead to hit the ball into center field.

3. Stride toward the plate if you want to knock it into the opposite field.

Even though these have all become options, I prefer to see a hitter remain in the stationary position, because there is less of a timing problem to cope with. Then all you need to do is get the timing down and stride with the front foot. There will be no worry about the actions of the rear foot, with both feet having a support base. Rotary side movements and weight transfer will accelerate the swinging arms to produce the power. But if the back foot is placed firmly and the front foot is not, then there will be a power loss from the double timing caused by each foot in different sequence. If you move the back foot toward the plate—as long as it and the front foot are placed on the ground—then you can start the top half swinging action.

The short (six-inch) stride is still most effective, and you must be careful not to overstride nor lunge at the ball. Remember, you can adjust the stride to the path of the ball in slow-pitch and, unlike fast-pitch, not depend solely on the hands and arms to take care of the bat while the feet remain stationary. Often a hitter will wait for a choice pitch, but there really never is any excuse to take a called third strike. I guess it rarely happens because the hitter can adjust to any pitch that is relatively close to the strike zone.

This technique may involve lifting your front knee and foot slightly straight up from the ground and then replanting the foot in the original spot. In fast-pitch, it takes an extraordinary hitter to make this movement and still be ready to hit a pitch that arrives in such a short period of time. Part of the reason is jarring the eye level away from the flight of the ball. But in slow-pitch the eyes will have time to refocus on the ball's path should they be thrown off course by lifting the front foot (remember, that action also lifts the body, including the head, and that is why the eyes may stray from the target).

The front knee coil action, while highly recommended only for an advanced fast-pitch hitter, is a great asset in slow-pitch and is a commonly used technique because it generates more power. The

FIGURE 10-1A

FIGURE 10-1E

FIGURE 10-1B

FIGURE 10-1F

FIGURE 10-1C

FIGURE 10-1D

FIGURE 10-1G

SLOW PITCH POWER SWING:
Because the speed of the pitch is reduced, the batter has more time to decide whether to take the pitch or swing, generate hip speed, and lengthen the arc of the swing. The latter two actions will help to generate additional power. The hands stay back (10-1C through 10-1E) until the front foot is planted (10-1F) and the rear foot exerts pressure on the ground, thus initiating and controlling both the lateral body movement "to go get the ball" and the "sit down" or squatting motion that allows the hips to rotate.

FIGURE 10-1H

PRONATION/SUPINATION: *In 10-1K through 10-1N the batter gets his top and bottom hands into the correct contatct position: the bottom*

FIGURE 10-1J

FIGURE 10-1I

hand pronating (or turning the palm downward) and the top hand supinating (or turning the palm upward). With this correct alignment

FIGURE 10-1K

FIGURE 10-1L

they can successfully whip the barrel of the bat through the contact, or
hitting, zone.

FIGURE 10-1N

FIGURE 10-1M

front knee coil action provides a linking action between the plant foot and the rear foot action of setting the lower leg slightly inwards. This creates force at the inside edge of the ball of the big toe. The initial action is to turn the front knee inwards laterally, so that only the front heel is slightly raised and pressure can be felt at the inside of the ball of the foot. Pressure may also be felt on the inside of the front knee, which insures the front hip rotating inwardly and prevents it from opening too soon.

Swinging the Bat

Swinging, of course, starts with the hands, and we covered the important points in Chapter VI. However, in slow-pitch hitting, the hands must go back much farther and wind up more. If the hands are too close to the body, they will have a tougher time getting into the necessary extension with power. Again because of the slower flight of the ball, you can hitch—drop the hands and then adjust them upward again—but both hands still must stay on the bat at all times. Often, that slowly pitched ball looks so juicy to hit that batters will almost unconsciously lift their top hand off the bat too soon before contact and thus lose the power they so dearly want to drive the pitch.

FIGURE 10-1O

FOLLOW THROUGH: The top hand does not roll over until a complete extension of the arms (10-1P Photo) and contact with the ball (Photo 10-1Q) have been made. Good head discipline keeps the head down,

FIGURE 10-1Q

FIGURE 10-1P

with the eyes concentrating on the oncoming ball throughout the entire swing.

The basic swinging technique in slow-pitch is slightly upward without dropping the end of the bat barrel too far. You really want to make contact with the ball around shoulder level, and anything lower requires dropping the bat and using an uppercut swing. If you wait until the ball is in the middle of your body—unless you are a line drive hitter—you will have to come underneath it with the uppercut swing, and it will be more difficult to lift the ball. If the ball drops below belt level before swinging, then you really must drop the bat barrel to get the pitch, again with a loss of power and perhaps too many fly balls and pop ups, or you'll end up swinging down and contact just the top of the ball for a weak grounder.

Since slow-pitch hitting is basically a power-hitting exercise, you can coil the shoulders more by turning the upper half of the body to a greater degree than in fast-pitch hitting, still keeping the angles of the arms the same with the shoulder. You also can raise the knee slightly to keep the front hip closed so when the front foot is planted, more power will be produced. The shoulders can be rotated inwardly to an almost exaggerated degree because there is time to uncoil with the stride of the front foot, which can be moved to any spot you desire. When you are coiling the shoulder, there will be a slight muscle contract or stretch in the front shoulder, as described in feel point 8.

The line drive hitter can wait for the ball to come down lower,

FIGURE 10-2A

FIGURE 10-2E

FIGURE 10-2B

FIGURE 10-2F

FIGURE 10-2C

FIGURE 10-2D

FIGURE 10-2G

MOVING IN THE STANCE TO PULL THE BALL/SLOW PITCH:
The batter assumes a square or slightly open stance in rear of the batter's box close to the edge of the plate (10-2A). As the ball is released, the batter determines where it will reach the plate area (in our sequence, we've pre-positioned the ball on a tee to simulate the batter's judgment) and moves his back foot into the new stance position with a short shuffle step. To pull the ball, the batter then "steps in the bucket," or toward foul territory to allow for a quicker rotary motion, or clearing, of the hips. This increases shoulder, arm and hand speed, and upon contact, generates more power.

FIGURE 10-3C

FIGURE 10-3D

FIGURE 10-3G

MOVING IN THE STANCE TO PULL THE BALL/SLOW PITCH:

This is the same movement shown in the preceding sequence, except in this sequence we get a better look at the shoulder coil (10-3E), which produces Feel Point #6 (a muscular contraction on the inside of the front shoulder and a muscular stretch at the outer part of the front shoulder). Our camera angle in 10-3E shows the bat wrapped around the rear shoulder and rear hip as it begins its rapid opening. This position will generate maximum power.

FIGURE 10-4A

FIGURE 10-4E

FIGURE 10-4B

FIGURE 10-4F

FIGURE 10-4C

FIGURE 10-4D

FIGURE 10-4G

MOVING IN THE STANCE TO HIT TO OPPOSITE FIELD/SLOW
PITCH: *The batter assumes a square stance in the rear and outside portion of the batter's box (10-4A and 10-4B). As the ball is released, the batter determines where it will reach the plate area (in our sequence, we've pre-positioned the ball on a tee to simulate the batter's judgment) and moves his back foot into the new stance position with a short shuffle step. To drive the ball to the opposite field, the batter then steps toward right centerfield. (10-4F). The hips, when fully opened (10-4G), are facing the intended hitting area.*

FIGURE 10-5A   **FIGURE 10-5B**

STARTING SWING WITH HANDS AT HIP LEVEL: *Dropping the hands to hip level for the start of the swing can help generate a pronounced shoulder turn (away from the oncoming pitch) and weight shift—both*

FIGURE 10-5E   **FIGURE 10-5F**

FIGURE 10-5C   **FIGURE 10-5D**

are aids in generating additional power (by increasing the speed of the hip rotation, which, in turn, increases the arm and hand speed through the contact area).

probably around belt level, before swinging. The line drive swing is more level.

Pivoting is the same in slow-pitch as it is in fast-pitch. It is a simple fact in baseball, as well as in both facets of softball, that the more force exerted against the ground while pivoting and the faster a hitter turns, the more power is generated for a pitch in the middle of the plate.

Hitting Adjustments for Slow-Pitch

Slow-pitch hitters are just as selective about where they want to hit the pitch as in any other type of baseball, and they have a better opportunity to fulfill those wishes because they have time to line up the pitch and make the necessary moves. Here are the four possibilities:

1. *Adjusting for the outside pitch.* Your hands must be ahead of the bat barrel, and your hips do not open as far as on an inside pitch. The rear shoulder will finish in line with the direction in which the pitch has been hit. The toes of the rear foot as well as the rear hip and shoulder will be pointing toward opposite fields. For foot action, either

keep the feet fixed or stride toward the plate to hit to the opposite field.

2. *Adjusting for the inside pitch.* Place the front foot toward the pull side of the plate and hit the ball down the line. The rear shoulder will replace the front shoulder.

3. *Adjusting for the letter-high pitch.* You have three choices in making contact with a ball slightly below your shoulder level, but the first two are best for power hitters. The first is to bring the hands slightly forward and downward while turning the thumb side of the bottom hand downward. This movement positions the barrel back and below the hands. As a result, a larger arc and longer path for the barrel is created to generate power to contact the pitch.

The second method is lowering the hands and the bat straight downward to the hip level, turning the bottom hand down and creating a much greater arc and path for power. Both of these swings are of the uppercut variety.

If you're not a power hitter, you should wait for the pitch to get a little lower and have your hands lower than the barrel. This is the third style. That swing is taken with a slight downward motion, producing either a line drive or ground ball.

4. *Adjusting for the low pitch.* The slow-pitch hitter, as we noted earlier, must uppercut the ball if it is at waist level or below belt level.

Regardless of the pitch, a ball thrown with a higher arc will come down faster, so timing is very important for each type of hitter.

About the Authors

TOM PETROFF

Veteran baseball coach Tom Petroff is currently an assistant coach at the University of Iowa. A former pro baseball player, he was recently inducted into the NCAA Coaches Hall of Fame. Petroff was the College Division Coach of the Year in 1972 while head coach at the University of Northern Colorado. He coached the U.S. Amateur Team at the World Games in Seoul, Korea (1982) and at the World Friendship Series in Newark, Ohio (1981) and was elected President of the American Baseball Coaches Association in 1984. He is renowned for his teaching skills and has conducted more than 60 clinics across the country during his long and distinguished career. Tom's recent book, *Baseball Signs and Signals*, which appeals to all ages, was chosen by The New York Public Library as one of the best books of the year for teenagers.

JACK CLARY

Freelance writer Jack Clary has co-authored, written and edited more than two dozen books on a variety of sports subjects during some 30 years as a journalist. He has authored books with NFL Hall of Famers Paul Brown (*PB*) and Andy Robustelli (*Once a Giant, Always...*) as well as with former Bengals quarterback Ken Anderson (*The Art of Quarterbacking*); and current Minnesota Twins batting coach Tony Oliva (*Youth League Hitting Like a Champ*). Some other books include *Great Moments in Pro Football, Careers in Sports, Army vs. Navy and The Gamemakers* with such renowned coaches as Tom Landry, John Madden, Chuck Noll, Don Shula and others. In addition to working as a consultant in his firm, Sports Media Enterprise, Clary spent 17 years as a sportswriter and columnist for The Associated Press, *New York World Telegram & Sun* and the *Boston Herald Traveler*.

Credits

Book Production/Design: Mountain Lion, Inc.
Cover Design: Michael Bruner
Copyediting: Deborah Crisfield
Photographs: Michael Plunkett
Typesetting: Elizabeth Typesetting Company
Mechanical: Production Graphics
Cover Photograph: Focus on Sports, Inc.